Little Mac Word Book

Helmut Kobler

Peachpit Press
Berkeley ▾ California

The Little Mac Word Book
Helmut Kobler

Peachpit Press, Inc.
2414 Sixth Street
Berkeley, California 94710
(800) 283.9444
(510) 548.4393
(510) 548.5991 fax

Copyright © 1992 by Helmut Kobler
Cover design by Studio Silicon

All rights reserved. No part of this book may be reproduced or transmitted in any form or by any means, electronic, mechanical, photocopying, recording, or otherwise, without the prior written permission of the publisher.
For information, contact Peachpit Press, Inc.

Notice of Liability
The information in this book is distributed on an "As is" basis, without warranty. While every precaution has been taken in the preparation of this book, neither the author nor Peachpit Press, Inc., shall have any liability to any person or entity with respect to any liability, loss, or damage caused or alleged to be caused directly or indirectly by the instructions contained in this book or by the computer software and hardware products described herein.

Trademarks
Throughout this book trademarked names are used. Rather than put a trademark symbol in every occurrence of a trademarked name, we state we are using the names only in an editorial fashion and to the benefit of the trademark owner with no intention of infringement of the trademark.

ISBN 0-938151-87-8

0 9 8 7 6 5 4 3 2

Printed and bound in the United States of America

To Mom. I love you!

Thank You!

More than a few people have helped me throughout this project. Foremost, I'd like to thank Ted Nace, publisher of Peachpit Press, for his expertise, hand-holding, and patience. The entire Peachpit staff has also been a great help, letting me tap their sharp book-sense, and being good friends as well.

I must also thank Robin Williams, author of the one and only *Little Mac Book* (and other fine titles), for providing me with this book's beautiful design; Kimn Neilson, for her sharp editing eye; and Mary Grady, for a thorough index.

Thanks also to David Pearce and others at Microsoft, for technical expertise, and for delivering much-needed beta software and manuals. I would have been lost without this support.

Thanks to Treanna Clinton and Lois Kobler for reading the manuscript with a real-world, end user's perspective; also to the gang at Asher House for their frequent input on cover designs, not to mention late-night cookie breaks.

Finally, thanks to Leigh, for turning a very hectic semester into something special.

Contents

What's New with 5.0 9
A quick survey of Word 5.0's many new features, along with where to look for more in-depth explanations.

Project Guide 15
You'd like to create a certain type of document, but aren't sure which of Word's features will be helpful. Here's a list of everyday document projects and the appropriate Word tools to help accomplish them.

1 Word Basics 19
    Requirements and Installation 20
    Starting a Document 22
    Page Breaks in Your Document 27
    Viewing Your Document 29
    Opening, Saving, and Finding Documents 33
    Printing Your Document 38
    Word's Document Windows 39
    Operating Word from the Keyboard 41
    Getting Online Help 42

2 Formatting Text 45
    Word's Ruler and Ribbon 46
    Setting Margin Indents and Tabs 50
    The Character Command 53
    The Paragraph Command 55
    Numbering Lines and Paragraphs 58
    Styles and the Style Sheet 61
    Making Tables 64

Contents

3 Setting Up a Document 71
Sections in a Document 72
Setting Page Size, Orientation, and Margins 74
Setting Up Columns 76
Page Numbers 77
Headers and Footers 78

4 Writing and Editing Tools 81
The Spelling Checker 82
The Grammar Checker 85
The Thesaurus 89
Hyphenation 90
Word Count 91
Find and Replace 92
Glossaries for Quick Text and Graphics 96

5 Working with Graphics 101
Fundamentals: Graphics Frames and Positioning 102
Word's Built-In Drawing Program 104
Importing Graphics from Other Programs 109
Manipulating Graphics—Cropping, Scaling, and More ... 111
Simpler Graphics—Borders, Rules, and Shading 111

6 Book and Reference Tools 117
Making a Table of Contents 118
Making an Index 125
Automatic Footnotes 131
Outlining with Word 137
Linking Documents in a Series 144

7 Miscellaneous Stuff 147
Positioning Text and Graphics 148
Making Voice Annotations 153
Math Calculations 156
Sorting Information 157
Print Merge for Form Letters and Mailing Labels 158
Merging with Mailing Labels 166
Math and Scientific Equations 167

8 Printing Your Documents 171

Setting Up Your Printer 172
Printing Basics 173
Setting Up Pages for Printing 176
Printing with Different Printers 180
Printing Envelopes 182
Printing PostScript Disk Files 184
Printing Linked Documents 185

9 Sharing Information with Other Programs 187

Sharing Information the Easy Way 188
Publishing and Subscribing 191
Linking Documents and Other Programs 195
Embedding Information 197
Linking Information with System 6 199
Opening and Saving Documents in Other File Formats 200
Placing Word Documents in Other Programs 203

10 Customizing Word 205

Word's Default Settings 206
Customizing Menus and Keyboard Commands 210
Saving Your Customizations 213

Keyboard Shortcuts 215

When you become comfortable with Word, you'll want to start using some of its many keyboard shortcuts for greater efficiency. (Keyboard shortcuts are quicker alternatives to pointing, clicking, and dragging the mouse.) Here's a list of many of Word's more useful key commands.

Index 219

What's New with 5.0

If you're already familiar with *Word* 4.0, you'll want to get going right away with 5.0's new features. There are dozens of changes to this latest edition of *Word*, many of them minor. For instance, you're bound to notice a revamped interface—some familiar menus have been renamed, menu items moved to different spots, dialog boxes modified, and a few features have even been renamed. The old Position command of 4.0 is a prime example, since it's now become Frame in 5.0. Nonetheless, if you're already familiar with *Word* 4.0, it should take you all of five minutes to get acquainted with 5.0.

I won't go through every changed facet of the software, then, but I'll cover the major additions that affect how you work with *Word*. I'll also provide page numbers for each new feature listed, so you can quickly look them up here and get the details you need.

Drawing Tools

Word now offers basic drawing tools such as lines, arrow pointers, ellipses, rectangles, arcs, and fill patterns, plus extra features like graphic rotation, image mirroring, and more. You probably won't want to abandon your dedicated drawing packages (*MacDraw*, *Canvas*, etc.) but *Word's* drawing tools are nonetheless handy for producing simple illustrations, and making quick edits to imported graphics. Page 104.

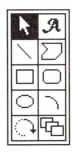

A sample of Word's new drawing tools.

Find and Replace

Word has always had a find and replace feature, but 5.0 now lets you easily find and replace text attributes in your documents, such as specific fonts and point sizes, bold or italic styles, paragraph formats, style sheet styles, and more. For instance, you can tell *Word* to find all text formatted in New Baskerville, Italic, at 12 points, and change those occurrences to Futura Book, Bold, at 10 points. The find and replace feature also makes it easier to work with special characters, such as tabs, page breaks, and wild card characters. Page 92.

What's New with 5.0

Grammar Checking

Just as *Word* can check your documents for spelling errors, it can now look for grammar problems, such as bad subject and verb agreement, pronoun errors, double negatives, wordiness, poor punctuation, and more. This doesn't mean *Word* can crank out polished prose for you—grammar-checking technology still needs a little fine-tuning, apparently—but the new grammar checker does help eliminate some of the careless, sloppy writing that we're all known to produce. Page 85.

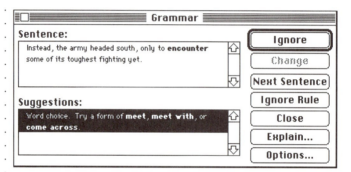

The new grammar checker. It works a lot like Word's spelling checker in that it scans your prose and makes suggestions for improvement. You can take its advice or leave it.

Border Maker

Word has a new feature devoted to creating graphic borders, frames, and line rules for text, tables, and graphics in your documents. You can choose from a variety of border line styles, and apply background shading to bordered elements. Page 111.

Equation Editor

If your documents call for scientific and mathematical equations, you no longer have to create them with *Word's* arcane math typesetting language. Instead, the new Equation Editor lets you conveniently choose prebuilt equation symbols and expressions from a large library, and then type in whatever numbers and variables you'd like. Page 167.

Print Merge Helper

Word's print merge feature is now easier to use, thanks to 5.0's Print Merge Helper. The Helper makes it much more convenient to set up the main and data documents for your print merge—for instance, you can quickly

What's New with 5.0

enter and delete data field names in a simple dialog box, and insert field names and print merge commands by way of a special, Ruler-like command bar. Page 166.

The Ribbon

Like *Word's* familiar Ruler, the new Ribbon sits at the top of your document window and gives you quick and easy access to some of *Word's* most common formatting features. For instance, you can use the Ribbon to choose fonts and point sizes, and styles such as bold, italic, and underline. The Ribbon also lets you change the number of columns in your document with a quick click of an icon. Page 46.

Word's Ribbon sits at the top of your document window, and makes formatting text more convenient (among other things).

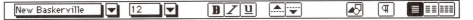

Thesaurus

Word 4.0 included a separate desk accessory thesaurus called *WordFinder*, but the thesaurus feature is built directly into *Word* 5.0. Besides, *Word's* new thesaurus is more adept at suggesting synonyms and similar meanings for words, and now offers antonyms, too. Page 89.

Voice Annotations

If you've got a Macintosh with a built-in microphone (as Classic II's, LC's, IIsi's and all newer models do), or if you have an add-on microphone such as Farallon's MacRecorder, then you can record voice annotations in your documents. For instance, you could leave a voice annotation for your editor, such as "Mary, do you think this paragraph needs further explanation?" While your Mac needs a microphone to record such annotations, any Mac can play them back. Page 153.

If your Mac features a microphone, you can spice up documents with voice recordings—for instance, "Bob, see if you can tighten up this passage. I wrote it with a hang-over!"

WHAT'S NEW WITH 5.0

Find File

Do you spend too much time searching your hard drive's folders for *Word* documents and other related files? *Word's* new Find File feature helps locate files on your disk, letting you search by a number of criteria such as file type (*Word* documents, graphics files, *Excel* spreadsheets, etc.), file date and time, and more. You can even search for documents that contain specific text, such as "Out, damned spot! Out, I say!" What's more, Find File is blazingly fast. Page 36.

Ever misplace a document, and then have to sift through folder after folder to find it? Ta da! The new Find File tracks down all sorts of files in just moments.

Summary Information

You can now save your *Word* documents with summary information, giving each one an official title, and identifying it by subject, author name, and keywords to help distinguish it. This is especially handy if you share documents with a number of people—copy writers and editors in a workgroup, perhaps—and want to better identify the various documents the group works with. Page 36.

Drag and Drop Text Editing

You can move text around in your document without using *Word's* Cut, Copy, and Paste commands. Just highlight the text, and click and drag the selection to a new point in your document. Page 25.

WHAT'S NEW WITH 5.0

Plug-In Modules

You can now add new features to *Word* by way of plug-in modules—these are special command files that you place in *Word's* folder on your hard disk. Many of *Word's* current features are already in the form of plug-in modules, such as spell checking, voice annotations, and online help. In the future, you'll be able to buy other plug-ins —for instance, a company called Niles and Associates will provide a module to manage bibliographic citations . Microsoft itself will also enhance *Word* through plug-in modules—look for a Macro module that lets you automate many of the tasks you do in *Word*. Page 21.

New Preferences

Word now features a much more extensive Preferences command, which lets you set a wide variety of custom default settings for the program. For instance, you can tell *Word* to open all documents with the Ruler and Ribbon features turned on, or to always make a backup of the documents you're working with. Page 206.

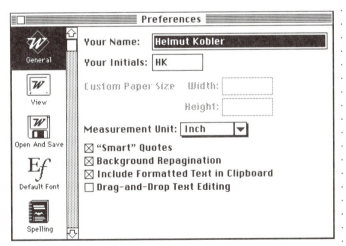

Word's new Preferences window lets you customize many of the program's options and features, from turning on Smart Quotes to automatically creating backups of your documents.

Recently Opened Documents

A minor but nonetheless convenient feature is *Word's* ability to list under its File menu the last four documents you worked with—select such a document from the menu, and *Word* opens it immediately. By listing these

13

documents under the File menu, they become easier to get at. Page 35.

System 7 Savvy

Word 5.0 now takes full advantage of Apple's System 7 operating system—that is, if you've installed this sophisticated system on your Macintosh. Most important of *Word's* System 7 features is Publish and Subscribe, which lets *Word* share information with other programs, and automatically update that information if it changes in its original source. For instance, you can place an *Excel* pie chart in your *Word* business report—if that pie chart is ever updated in *Excel*, the change is reflected in your *Word* document as well. You don't have to manually re-cut and paste the new information back. Page 191.

Word also supports System 7's TrueType "outline" fonts, which print super crisp and clean (on both paper and your screen), no matter what size the characters are. And finally, there's Balloon Help, which gives brief explanations of the menu items, dialog box options, and other *Word* elements that you point your mouse at. Page 43.

Project Guide

Sometimes you'll know exactly what you want to do with *Word*—create a newsletter, or draft a business report, for instance—but you won't know which features will be helpful in that task. These next few pages are for you. Here I list some common projects that *Word* is often recruited for, and give you a quick run down of which features may be helpful to know, and where in this book you can learn more about them.

Just Trying to Figure Out the Program

If you're new to *Word*, or word processing altogether, I recommend starting with chapter one, *Word Basics*. I explain *Word's* fundamentals there, from typing in text to viewing documents on-screen to printing to keyboard shortcuts. With these fundamentals under your belt, you can move on to the book's other chapters, which give you a feel for the program in greater detail.

Simple Letter Writing and Correspondence

Not much here. Just be familiar with the basics of entering and formatting text (page 46), and perhaps a few of *Word's* writing tools, such as the spelling and grammar checkers (page 82, 85). You might also want to brush up on printing envelopes with your dot-matrix or laser printer (page 182).

Creating or Importing Graphics

It would be a good idea to read all of chapter five, *Working with Graphics*, which explains how to use *Word's* new drawing tools to make graphics from scratch, as well as how to import graphics from any other applications you use. Chapter five ends with a talk about *Word's* Border feature, which lets you add borders, frames and background shading to text and graphics in your document. You might want also refer to page 148, which explains how to position your graphics anywhere on a document's page.

Page Layout for Newsletters, Brochures, Etc.

If you want to use *Word* as a page layout program, then you'll want to know how to set up multiple columns (page 76), how to position text and graphics anywhere on the page (page 148), and how to highlight these elements with borders, frames, and background shading (page 111). You should also brush up on *Word's* Section feature (page 72), which lets you divide your document into different, uniquely formatted parts (so, for instance, you can have varying column layouts or different page margins in the same document).

Tables of Data

You *don't* want to use *Word's* tab markers to set up tables of text and numbers in your documents. Instead, there's a handy Table feature (page 64) that makes creating and adjusting tables quick and painless (relatively, of course). If your tables incorporate data from another application—a spreadsheet file from *Lotus 1-2-3*, or database information out of *FoxBASE*, perhaps—then see page 187 for how to incorporate information from such sources. Pay particular attention to the Publish and Subscribe feature (page 191), which lets *Word* share and automatically update data from other programs (your Mac needs to run the System 7 operating system to work with Publish and Subscribe, however). Finally, *Word's* Sort command (page 157) can help you arrange table data in an alphabetical or numeric order.

Books and Other Long Documents

If you're tackling long, complex documents, the first place to turn is chapter six, *Book and Reference Tools*, which explains many of *Word's* most appropriate features. For instance, you might want to start organizing your documents with the Outline feature, which helps develop your ideas and arrange their delivery. *Word's* Table of Contents and Index generation features are also useful for creating references to your work, as is the automatic Footnote feature for documenting ideas. Check out *Word's* Paragraph Numbering ability (page 58) for establishing a hierarchy in a long document's various sections and headings; and try Headers and

Footers (page 78) for printing repeating information, like chapter titles, on every page.

It's also a good idea to know *Word's* Section feature, which lets you divide a document into differently formatted parts. And don't even attempt a long document without using *Word's* Style Sheets (page 61) to automate text formatting and the inevitable formatting revisions that come later.

Finally, if you're creating really big projects, you might want to divide chapters or sections into multiple documents, to keep file size down and to keep *Word* running smoothly. You can link these multiple documents together so they print as one continuous piece, however (page 144).

Form Letters and Mailing Labels

For print merging form letters and mailing labels, see page 158. That's where you'll find all the basics you need to know for tackling these complex projects.

Business Reports with Financial Data

Business reports are likely to include tables of data, so read up on *Word's* handy Table feature (page 64). You might also want to read a bit of chapter nine, which explains how to bring information into *Word* from other programs—you might need this, for instance, for copying charts, graphs, or spreadsheet information into your document. If your Mac is running Apple's System 7 operating system, look closely at the Publish and Subscribe feature (page 191), which automates the sharing of information between *Word* and other applications. And if you want to position those business graphics on your page in an attractive way (a la page layout programs such as *PageMaker*), then see page 148.

Working on a Network

If you use *Word* on a network with other people (co-editors and writers, for instance) then you'll definitely want to master the Publish and Subscribe feature (page 191), which lets you share and quickly update information with other users on the net. While you're sharing documents with your co-workers, it might also be helpful to include some voice annotations in your text (page 153). And don't neglect the new Summary Info feature (page 36), which let's you summarize the essential information about a document (so co-workers can distinguish each other's documents more easily).

Exchanging Documents with Other Word Processors

If you'd like to import documents created in other applications, such as *MacWrite* or *WordPerfect* on the PC, then see page 200 for the appropriate steps to take. The same goes if you're working the other way around—that is, moving Mac *Word* documents to other applications.

CHAPTER 1

Word Basics

What's Inside

- ▼ Requirements and Installation
- ▼ Starting a Document
- ▼ Page Breaks in Your Document
- ▼ Viewing Your Document
- ▼ Opening, Saving, and Finding Documents
- ▼ Printing Your Document
- ▼ Word's Document Windows
- ▼ Operating Word from the Keyboard
- ▼ Getting Online Help

Chapter One ▾ Word Basics

If you're new to *Microsoft Word*, or even just partially acquainted, then you're in the right place. This chapter is meant to give you an overview of how *Word* works, from typing and formatting text to saving document files to working with keyboard commands to finally printing. Once you've got a feel for the topics presented here, you can move on into the program, and also better understand the rest of the material in *The Little Mac Word Book*.

Requirements and Installation

Before delving into *Word* itself, we have just a few preliminaries to cover.

What You Need to Use Word

Word 5.0's basic Macintosh requirements are moderate. As a bare minimum set-up, you need any Macintosh from the Mac Plus and up (this includes the Classic, the SE, the LC, the Power Books, the Macintosh IIs, Quadras, and whatever other equipment Apple will undoubtedly churn out pretty soon). You also need a hard disk drive, with about six megabytes of free space, if you want to use all of *Word's* features and supplementary files. One megabyte of memory is a minimum, but you'll need two megabytes to run *Word* with its grammar checker, System 6's MultiFinder option, or the new System 7. Your Mac also needs to have System 6.02 (or higher) installed. If you don't have an up-to-date System, you can call your local Macintosh dealer—they're licensed to give you one. You don't *need* a printer, but I really recommend having one on hand to get the most out of this software.

Finally, let me just say that bare requirements aside, *Word* is a big, sophisticated program, and it may run a bit slow on some lower-end Macs like the Plus, SE, and Classic. If you doing a lot of writing, I'd recommend investing in an accelerator board to boost your computer's pace.

System 7. By the way, if you're not already using Apple's System 7 operating system, now might be a good time to try it. By now, most worthwhile Mac programs run, if not excel, with System 7. In particular, *Word* 5.0 gains a lot (see page 14 for its System 7-specific features). However, if System 7 is not an option for you—perhaps your Mac doesn't have the recommended 2 megabytes of RAM—then using System 6 is fine.

Installing Word

You can find detailed instructions for installing *Word* in your *Microsoft Word* manuals, but the procedure is so straightforward that you probably won't need any help. To summarize: of the 5 disks included in your *Word* package, insert the Install disk into your Mac, and double-click the Installer program on that disk. *Word* now walks you through the installation process—it asks a few questions, creates a new folder on your hard disk, prompts you for the remaining *Word* disks, and returns to your Mac's desktop when the installation is complete.

What's in the Word folder. You should be acquainted with the *Word* files installed on your hard drive. First and foremost is the Microsoft Word program file. It's by far the largest file in the Word folder, and you'll double-click it to start using *Word*. Other important files are contained by the Word Commands folder (also in the Word folder). These "plug-in modules" give *Word* many of its features, such as spell checking, equation editing, and online help. It's important that the plug-in modules stay in their folder, or else *Word* won't work properly.

Some of Word's plug-in modules. Make sure they're in the Word Commands folder.

The Word folder also features many sample and practice documents that help you get a feel for how *Word* works in a variety of jobs. Finally, there are also special settings and glossary files that you don't have to worry about until later in your work with *Word*.

Starting Word

To start *Word*, open the Word folder on your hard drive, and double-click the Microsoft Word program file. *Word* responds by loading itself into your Mac's memory and opening a new document window. If you've already created documents in *Word*, you can double-click these files—*Word* starts itself, and then opens the document you just clicked.

Double-click this file to launch Word 5.0.

You'll notice, by the way, that when *Word* starts, it displays a title screen including your name, company, and program serial number. This identifies the software as licensed to you—consequently, you may think twice before freely copying Word for your friends, associates, etc., since the circulating copies will carry your name.

STARTING A DOCUMENT

If you've just started Word from your Mac's desktop, then *Word* will have already opened a new document window for you to work with. If not, you can select New from the File menu to open a new document window. Notice that *Word* calls the document *Untitled1*—all new documents are called *Untitledx* (1, 2, 3, etc.), until you save them with a new name. See page 33 for details about saving.

Typing in Text

Typing text in *Word* is straightforward, but there are a few important things to remember as you go along.

Don't hit Return. You should not hit the Return key at the end of each line that you type (hard to believe if you're used to a conventional typewriter). As your typing approaches the right side of the document window, *Word* automatically wraps the text to the next line for you, without interrupting the typing process. You should only hit the Return key when you'd like to start typing on a new line altogether—for instance, when you're beginning a new paragraph.

Don't use the space bar. The second rule to remember is that you should not use the space bar to align, indent, or otherwise position text on a line—for instance, to center a heading on the page. Using the space bar for these tasks often makes your document print differently than you expected (usually for the worse). Instead, you can use *Word's* paragraph indent, tab, and alignment features to position text in any manner. We'll come to these in a moment.

Word Basics ▼ CHAPTER ONE

Positioning the text cursor. By the way, *Word* places the text you type at the point of the blinking text cursor on-screen. You can position this cursor anywhere in your document by moving *Word's* I-beam pointer around with your mouse. Move the I-beam to any point on screen, and click the mouse button to position the text cursor there. You can also move the cursor with your Mac's arrow keys, and other methods that I talk about in the section *Moving Around a Document*, below.

This is the I-beam pointer. Move it around the screen with your mouse, and use it to highlight text, or position the text cursor anywhere on-screen.

Who Are Those Weird Characters, Anyway?

You may notice that *Word* inserts strange looking characters into the document you're creating—for instance, it displays little dots where you've hit the space bar, and foreign ¶ symbols where you've hit Return. These are called "paragraph marks," and their purpose is to simply make it easier to see where there's a space, or Return, or Tab mark on your Mac's screen (note: even though you see them on-screen, they won't print in your documents). Some people like seeing these paragraph marks as they work—personally, I think they make the screen look a mess. To turn them off (or on again), choose Show ¶ from the *Word's* View menu.

Word's so-called "paragraph marks" help you identify spaces, Returns and tabs in your document. You can turn them on and off with the Show ¶ feature under the View menu.

CHAPTER ONE ▾ Word Basics

 Along with formatting text, you might also want to set custom page margins and page numbers for your document. See chapter three starting on page 71 for more information.

Formatting Text

Once you've typed in text, you'll want to format it in a particular font, size, or style, set its line spacing, its alignment (left, right, centered, etc.), or its tab settings. To make these and almost all other changes, first select the text to change. Position the I-beam pointer at the start of the text, and click and hold the mouse button. Now drag the mouse to the end of the desired text—notice how the text in between becomes highlighted—and release the button. Now you're ready for formatting.

The Ruler and Ribbon. *Word's* Ruler and Ribbon command bars sit at the top of your document window, and offer the most convenient way to do most of your text formatting. You can turn them on from the View menu.

The Ruler and Ribbon work similarly in that they offer menus and icons for *Word's* most common formatting features—you simply select your text, and then click the appropriate menu or icon on the Ruler or Ribbon. The Ruler also lets you set margin indents for your text, tabs stops, and also text alignment like Left, Right, Centered, and Justified. I explain these features more thoroughly on page 46.

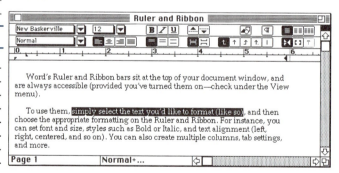

Word's Ribbon

Word's Ruler

Other formatting. *Word* offers many more formatting options than are covered by the Ruler and Ribbon. You can choose many of these by highlighting text, and then choosing either Character or Paragraph from the Format menu. I explain these features starting on page 53.

Moving Text in a Document—
Cut, Copy, Paste, Drag

There comes a time when you want to move a line, or paragraph, or any passage of text to a new place. To do this, select the text, and then choose either the Cut or Copy command from *Word's* Edit menu. Cut will remove the text selection from its current location, and store it in a section of your Mac's memory, called the Clipboard (page 188). Copy leaves the selection hhere it is, but makes a copy in the Mac's Clipboard.

Now position *Word's* text cursor in the spot where you'd like to move the text—don't position just the I-beam pointer, but the text cursor itself. Then choose Paste from the Edit menu to place the text in its new location. The text, by the way, stays in the Mac's Clipboard until you cut or copy new information there, so you can paste the same information as many times as you like.

Drag-and-Drop. *Word* 5.0 has a new shortcut for moving text without using Cut, Copy, and Paste. Highlight the range of text you'd like, and then click and hold the mouse pointer within the highlighted passage. *Word's* pointer becomes grayed on the bottom, indicating that you've "picked up" that text selection. Now drag the pointer to a new location in your document and release the mouse button to place the text. Some people find drag-and-drop handy; personally, I often drag and drop text by accident, when I only mean to select it. If you do the same, then you can disable the feature by choosing Preferences from the Tools menu and unchecking the Drag-and-Drop Text Editing option.

Undoing Your Mistakes

If you delete some text, or perform some command that doesn't produce the results you hoped, then choose the Undo command from Word's Edit menu (or press Command-Z). *Word* will graciously pretend you didn't perform the last action—for instance, a find and replace, positioning a graphic, or change in formatting.

Always keep in mind, however, that Undo only affects the last action you performed in *Word*, so you should use Undo immediately following an undesired action. If you

💡 *Many programs feature multiple levels of Undo, so you can backtrack through a number of previous commands and editing changes. Unfortunately, Word still undoes just the last action you've performed—no more.*

go on to perform other functions instead, Undo won't help in correcting a mistake you've made.

By the way, you can also redo an action that you undo. Choose Redo from the Edit menu (or type Command-Y).

Tips for Selecting Text

There are many different ways to select text in *Word*. The most common is to use the mouse to position *Word's* I-beam pointer at the beginning of the text you'd like to select, click and hold the mouse button, and then drag the mouse to highlight the selection.

Word also lets you select specific parts of text, such as whole words, paragraphs, or your entire document. To select the entire document—perhaps to change its font throughout—just choose Select All from the Edit menu (or press Command-A). To make more limited selections, position the I-beam over a word, and double-click the mouse to select the entire word. By triple-clicking, you'll select an entire paragraph. If you double- or triple-click, and then continue to hold the mouse button, you can drag the mouse to select a range of whole words or paragraphs.

You can also select text by using the keyboard. Hold down Shift and use the arrow keys to select text character by character, and line by line. Use Command-Shift to select word by word.

Selecting a large range of text. Sometimes you'll want to select a text spanning several screens or pages. To do this, first select a few words or lines at the beginning of the section. With that text highlighted, scroll through your document to the end of the section you want to select. Position the I-beam pointer at the end of the section, hold down the Shift key, and click the mouse. *Word* highlights all the text between the first selection, and this new point.

Moving Around a Document

You'll want to easily move around in any document you're creating—by move around, I mean position *Word's* text cursor to a new location in the document

> *To unselect text you've highlighted, just click the mouse.*

where you can type or select text. If you want to move the cursor to a new spot on the screen, you can use your keyboard's left/right, up/down arrow keys, or use the mouse to move *Word's* I-beam pointer to the appropriate spot, and click the button to place the text cursor at that point.

If you want to move to a part of the document that's not on-screen—the page above or below, for instance—then use the scroll bar on the right side of the document window. Click the bar's up and down arrows to scroll through the document one line at a time, or click the gray area of the bar to move one full screen at a time.

Moving by keyboard. You can also navigate through your document by keyboard, which is handy since you don't have to take your hands off the keyboard and interrupt typing. To move up by one full screen of text, hit 9 on the numeric keypad, or Page Up if you have an Extended Keyboard. Move down by hitting 3 on the numeric keypad, or Page Down. Likewise, you can jump to the very beginning of your document by hitting Command-9 (on the numeric keypad), or Command-Home with an Extended Keyboard. To move to the document's end, use Command-3, or Command-End.

> *You can move to a specific page in your document by choosing Go To from the Edit menu (or press Command-G), and typing the desired page number.*

PAGE BREAKS IN YOUR DOCUMENT

Pagination refers to *Word's* decision on where to put page breaks—that is, where to start a new page—in your document. *Word* automatically creates a new page when any text you're typing reaches the bottom of the current page. If you're working in *Word's* Normal view (more about *Word's* various view modes below), then these automatic page breaks appear as dotted horizontal lines that extend from one side of the screen to the other. In the Page Layout view, *Word* displays the actual pages on-screen, so it's obvious where one page ends and the next one begins.

CHAPTER ONE ▾ Word Basics

> formidable army—i:
> completely dwarfed
> **Page 6**
>
> *The lower-left corner of the document window tells which page you're working on.*

By the way, *Word* always displays the current page number you're working on in the lower left corner of the document window.

Controlling page breaks. Sometimes you'll want more control over where *Word* makes its page breaks—for instance, you'll want to create a new page for some important paragraph or section in your document. In this case, you can create a manual page break yourself, by positioning the text cursor at the appropriate spot (say, right above that important paragraph) and choosing Page Break from the Insert menu. You can delete this manual page break by simply backspacing over it with the text cursor.

You can also stop *Word* from breaking up important lines and paragraphs with a page break. See page 57 for details on how to do this with the Paragraph feature.

> *Here are examples of soft and hard (manual) page breaks.*

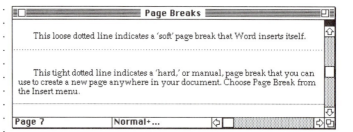

Repagination. When you add or delete text in your document, its page count and page breaks will naturally have to be revised. This is called Repagination, and *Word* can automatically repaginate your document through its Background Repagination feature—choose Preferences from the Tools menu, and turn the Background Repagination option on if it's not on already. If you're working with large, complex documents, however, this automatic repagination may slow *Word* down, so you might consider turning the Background Repagination off. In this case, you'll have to choose Repaginate Now from the Tools menu when you want to repaginate your document. No need to do this every time you edit text— just on the occasions when you want an accurate, up-to-date idea of the document's page count and page breaks.

Viewing Your Document

Word takes four different approaches to displaying your document on-screen, each specifically tuned for a unique advantage. *Word's* default view—the one it uses automatically—is its Normal view, which is ideal for writing, editing, and formatting your text. The Page Layout view, on the other hand, is better when you're doing layout in *Word*—for instance, working with multiple columns, or positioning graphics—since it displays your document on-screen exactly as it will print on paper. Likewise, *Word's* Print Preview gives a reduced view of your document, showing two full pages on-screen so you can easily check for page breaks, proper margins, headers and footers, and more. Finally, *Word's* Outline view is designed for showing your documents in a traditional outline format.

Let's look more closely at each view.

Normal View

The Normal view is the standard view that *Word* uses, and you can select it by choosing Normal from the View menu (or type Command-Option-N). This view is designed for composing the main text in your document,

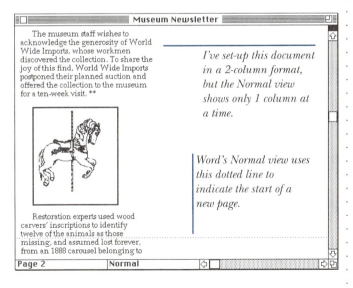

I've set-up this document in a 2-column format, but the Normal view shows only 1 column at a time.

Word's Normal view uses this dotted line to indicate the start of a new page.

Word's Normal view doesn't show graphics, multiple columns, headers/footers, footnotes or page numbers in their proper places, but it's the most efficient mode for writing and editing text.

Chapter One ▾ Word Basics

> 🔴 *Word's Normal and Page Layout views can seem a little sluggish if your Mac is running in color. To increase performance, use the Mac's Monitors control panel to set your Mac to Black and White mode.*

making it quick and easy to type, edit, and format text, and to move around through the document. Since it focuses on text, this view doesn't display your document exactly as it will print. For instance, the Normal view doesn't show true page margins, side-by-side columns, page numbers, headers and footers, footnotes, or graphics that you might position on the page. This isn't as limiting as it might seem, since you can switch to Page Layout or Print Preview views to see these items in place. In fact, you'll probably appreciate Normal view because it doesn't bog down by displaying these extras, but lets you concentrate on entering and formatting text.

Page Layout View

Choose Page Layout from the View menu (or type Command-Option-P) for *Word's* Page Layout view. Like *Word's* Normal view, you can edit and format text here, but Page Layout also displays each page as it will print—that means all elements, such as footnotes, multiple columns, and graphics are in their proper places. Some people prefer this What-You-See-Is-What-You-Get approach, and it's very useful hhen your documents

Word's Page Layout view shows multiple columns, graphics, headers/footers, footnotes and page numbers in their proper place, and lets you edit these elements as well. However, using this view can slow Word down slightly.

Click these arrows to change pages in the document.

30

require sophisticated layouts—a newsletter, for instance. For everyday work, however, I find this view distracting. It slows Word down a bit besides.

Note: If you *do* prefer the Page Layout view, you can set *Word* to use it as its default view. Choose Preferences from the Tools menu, select the View icon, and check the Open Documents In Page Layout View option.

Print Preview

Choose Print Preview from *Word's* File menu (or type Command-Option-I) for the Print Preview view. This is a unique view in that it doesn't let you edit text. However, since it shows one or two reduced pages on-screen, Print Preview makes it easy to check that page breaks, headers, footers, footnotes, graphics, and margins are in the best position. It gives you the best feel for a page's complete look. If you see a dubious item—perhaps a poorly positioned graphic—then you can either use Print Preview's magnifying glass to zoom in on that area of the page, or click the Page Layout button to go to that view mode, and make any corrections or adjustments.

Adjusting a page. You can also use Print Preview to adjust the layout of your pages. For instance, you easily place page numbers in your document—click the page number icon (the second icon from the top of the Print

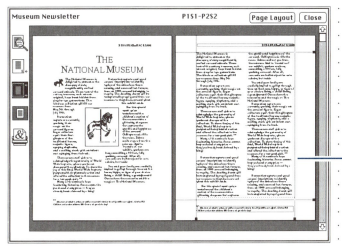

The Print Preview (under the File menu) shows reduced versions of your pages so you can make sure everything is in its proper place. You can't edit your document in this view, however.

Drag these margin guides (by their handles) to adjust your entire document's page margins.

Chapter One ▾ Word Basics

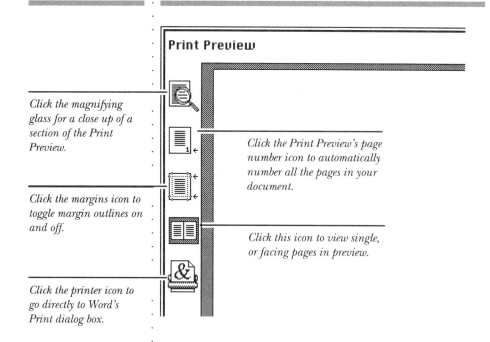

Click the magnifying glass for a close up of a section of the Print Preview.

Click the Print Preview's page number icon to automatically number all the pages in your document.

Click the margins icon to toggle margin outlines on and off.

Click this icon to view single, or facing pages in preview.

Click the printer icon to go directly to Word's Print dialog box.

Preview window), move the page number symbol to the appropriate place on a reduced page, and click the mouse. *Word* automatically numbers all of your pages in the spot you've just indicated (see page 77 for more about page numbers, by the way). You can also set a document's page margins by dragging the horizontal and vertical margin guides. Likewise, you can click and hold the mouse button within the borders of a header or footer, and adjust their position from the edges of the page. *Word* waits a moment or two, and applies these changes to all the pages in your document.

Outline View

Choosing Outline from the View menu (or typing Command-Option-O) brings you to *Word's* Outline view. Unlike the other views, you'll only use this view if you're organizing and developing a document based on an outline. I explain how to do this starting on page 137.

OPENING, SAVING, AND FINDING DOCUMENTS

If you have any Macintosh experience whatsoever, you'll already know the basics of opening and saving.

Saving Documents

There are two commands for saving *Word* documents—use the Save As command to save a new document for the first time, and the Save command to save changes to that document from then on.

Saving the first time. Choose Save As from the File menu, and *Word* calls up its save file dialog box. Type the name of the document into the Save Current Document As box. You may also want to select the specific folder to save this file in. The current folder is listed on the folder button at the top of the dialog box. You can select folders within this folder by browsing the file listing scroll box, or move to the main directory of your hard drive by clicking the folder button.

Also notice the dialog box's Save File as Type button. *Word* is able to save your documents in a format that

> ❗ *You can set many different open and save options by choosing Word's Preferences command under the Tools menu, and then clicking the Open and Save icon. See page 207.*

Click this button to navigate through folder levels on your hard drive.

This button reads "Drive" if your Mac is running System 6. Click it to list the contents of your Mac's other disk drives. System 6 Macs won't display the New Folder button either.

Click this button to choose the file format you'd like to save your document in.

many other word processors can understand, such as *WordPerfect* or *MacWrite II*. You can click this button to see and choose one of these many formats (for an explanation of these file formats, see page 200). If you don't plan to use your document in another word processor, however, leave this option at Normal.

Finally, notice the two options Fast Save and Make Backup. Checking Fast Save means that *Word* saves your document quickly, but the file takes up about 20% more space on your hard disk than normal. If Make Backup is checked, *Word* automatically saves a duplicate of your file, titled "Backup of *filename*" just in case something goes wrong with the original.

When you're ready, click the Save button to save your new document to disk. Before saving, though, you'll notice that *Word* opens a new dialog box, and prompts you for some summary information about your document. You don't have to fill in the information, but it may be helpful in some cases. See the section *Summarizing a Document*, below.

Saving subsequent times. Once you've saved a document and given it a proper name, you can choose Save from the File menu to append any changes you make to a document. *Word* saves only the new adds or deletes you've made, which quickens the saving process. This is known as "fast save," by the way.

When you use the Save command repeatedly, your document files can get larger than normal. To avoid this, use the Save As command every once in a while, and make sure the Fast Save option is not checked. Save the document under its same name, and *Word* will save the file at its proper size.

Opening Existing Documents

To open a presaved document, choose Open from the File menu, and *Word* responds with its open file dialog box. Find your document by selecting the Mac's main disk directory, or a folder, and scrolling through its file list. Click the appropriate file name, and then click the Open button (double-clicking the file name does the same thing).

Word Basics ▼ CHAPTER ONE

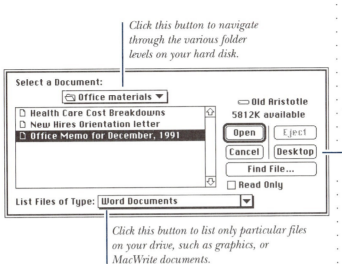

Click this button to navigate through the various folder levels on your hard disk.

The Open file box is fairly straightforward. Just select a file and click the Open button.

This button reads "Drive" if you use System 6. Click it to list the contents of your Mac's other disk drives.

Click this button to list only particular files on your drive, such as graphics, or MacWrite documents.

Listing particular files. You can click the List Files of Type button and select a category of files that *Word* will display in its open file box. For instance, choosing Graphic Files means that *Word* only lists files in that group, and nothing else, whereas Readable Files lists all the possible files that *Word* can work with. It's a convenient feature that makes sorting through long lists of files easier.

Finding a file. You can also click the Find File button, which lets you search your hard disk for a particular file or file type. See the section, *Finding Files*, below.

Recently opened documents. If you have a large computer screen (anything more than 9 inches), then *Word* lists the last four opened documents under the File menu, where you can select them quickly. It's a convenient feature, but if it bothers you for some reason (for instance, by cluttering your File menu) then you can turn it off by choosing Preferences from the Tools menu, selecting the View icon, and unchecking the List Recently Opened Documents option. Likewise, if you use a Mac with a smaller screen, but want to give this feature a try, use the Preferences command to turn the option on.

Through Word's Summary Info feature, you can identify a document by title, subject and information. Being able to so distinguish documents is especially helpful if you share your documents in a workgroup of people.

```
┌─────────────── Summary Info ───────────────┐
│  Title:     [Alexander of Macedon:1  ]  ( OK )    │
│  Subject:   [Alexander's boyhood     ]  (Cancel)  │
│  Author:    [Helmut Kobler           ]            │
│  Version:   [Draft                   ]            │
│  Keywords:  [Alexander, Youth        ]            │
└────────────────────────────────────────────┘
```

Summarizing a Document

You can save your documents with summary information, giving the document an official title, and identifying it by subject, author name, and keywords that help describe it. This is especially handy if you share documents with a number of people—copy writers and editors, perhaps—and want to better identify the various documents the group works on. Including summary information in a document is also helpful if you ever use *Word's* new Find File feature to locate the document on a crowded hard disk (more on this below).

Word automatically opens its Summary dialog box when you save a document for the first time. Just type in the relevant information, and hit OK when finished. That information becomes embedded in the document, and can be reviewed and updated by choosing Summary Info from the File menu any time thereafter.

Turning Summary Info on and off. You can set *Word* so that it doesn't automatically ask for summary information about a new document. Choose Preferences from the Tools menu, select the Open and Save icon, and uncheck the Prompt for Summary Info option. You can still manually enter a summary, however, by choosing Summary Info from the File menu.

Finding Files

Word 5.0 now has a powerful file search feature that helps track down documents and related files on your hard drive. To use it, choose Find File from the File menu. If you're in an open file dialog box, you can also click the Find File button. Either approach calls up *Word's* Search dialog box.

The Find File feature uses a variety of criteria to search for files on disk—for instance, it can find files by their name, by any summary information that you might have assigned through *Word's* Summary Info command, by file type such as graphics or *MacWrite* documents, and by the dates the files were created and last saved. *Word* even searches for text within a document—for instance, you can tell it to find a document that includes the phrase "sally sells sea shells" or any other text.

To search for a file, you don't have to enter criteria in every category—use only the categories you know, and leave the others blank. For instance, you may not remember the name of a particular document, but you do remember creating it sometime last week. In that case, you'd enter a Created From and Created To date.

When you click the OK button, *Word* opens a new dialog box and lists all the files it finds, their location on your disk drive, and other information. Select any file and click the Open button to bring the document, graphic, etc., into *Word*.

! *Try to narrow down searches as much as possible, so Find File doesn't have to peruse so many files (which takes more time, of course). For instance, specify a file type for the document you're searching, or enter a range of dates that the file was created within.*

The Find File box.

If the document you're searching contains unusual text, type it in here, and Word will search for that specific reference.

If you saved a document with summary information (see facing page), you can search for the elements of that summary.

You can narrow down the search by specifying a range of dates that a file was created or last saved within.

CHAPTER ONE ▼ Word Basics

Word lists all the files it's found here.

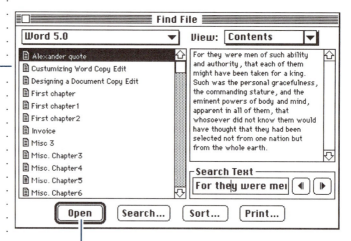

Select a file and click Open to open that document. The Search button brings you back to the main Find File box, while Sort sorts found files in alphabetical order. And the Print button prints a selected file.

PRINTING YOUR DOCUMENT

Before printing your document, you might want to use *Word's* Print Preview view to make sure that your pages look right (more about Print Preview on page 31). If everything checks out, choose Print from the File menu. You can type in the number of copies you want, as well as a page range to print, if you don't want to print the whole document. Then click the Print button.

Try to browse, if not read, chapter 8. *Word* supports many printing options that may be helpful to you, and these are explained there. The chapter also offers advice on how to avoid some common printing pitfalls.

Type in a page range, or the All option, and you're ready to print. See page 171 for more about printing your documents.

Word Basics ▾ CHAPTER ONE

WORD'S DOCUMENT WINDOWS

There are a few helpful things to know about the windows that *Word* uses to hold your documents. First is that *Word* can work with up to 8 different document windows at once (you can open the document by using the Open command under the File menu). This is really handy since it lets you easily compare one document to another, as well as move text between windows by using *Word's* Copy, Cut, and Paste commands. As with the Macintosh's Finder, only one open window stays "active" while the others remain in the background. You can activate a window by clicking it, or by pulling down *Word's* Window menu, and selecting from the menu's list of open documents. Like most other Macintosh windows, you can resize *Word's* document windows by clicking and dragging the Size box in the lower right corner of the window. You can also move the window around the screen by clicking and dragging in the Title bar on top. Using these features, you can position windows side by side so you can compare their contents and easily switch between them.

You can use Word's Window menu to "activate" any documents already opened.

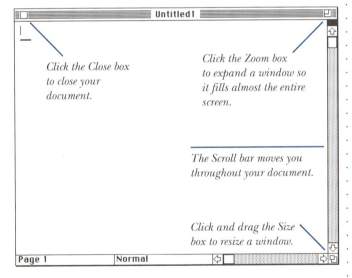

Anatomy of a document window.

Splitting a window into panes. You can split a document window into two separate parts—or "panes"—which lets you view different parts of your document at once. To

39

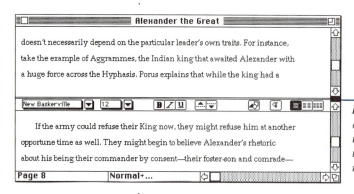

Drag the Split bar to create separate panes in the same window. Notice that each pane can have its own Ribbon or Ruler.

split a window into two panes, click and drag the black Split bar that sits directly above the upwards scroll arrow button. Drag the bar down into the window—notice the gray horizontal line that indicates the bar's position—and release the mouse button at the desired spot. Your document is now divided into two panes, where each pane lets you scroll and edit text in different areas of the same document. You can even set each pane to work in a different view mode—for instance, the top might display your document in W*ord's* Outline view, while the bottom is set to Normal. To set a pane's view, make sure *Word's* text cursor is in that pane, and then choose the desired view from the View menu.

To remove the split and make your window whole again, just drag the Split bar back on top of the upwards scroll arrow button on the window's Scroll bar. As a shortcut, you can also double-click the Split bar to make the window whole.

Viewing a document in multiple windows. Rather than split a window into two smaller panes, you might want to view the same document in multiple windows. To do this, make sure the document window you want to duplicate is active, and then choose New Window from the Window menu. *Word* responds by opening a new window containing the same document. You can edit and save in either window, and *Word* will automatically reflect the changes in the other window.

Operating Word from the Keyboard

Word, like most Mac applications, allows you to select many of its commands by typing key combinations, so you don't have to take your hands from the keyboard to grab the mouse. A key combination, by the way, is when you hold down a key such as Option, or the Command (Apple symbol) key, and simultaneously hit another character. You'll find key combinations listed next to their respective commands on *Word's* various pull-down menus. Next time you select a command by mouse, check to see if it has a corresponding keyboard shortcut.

More Keyboard Controls

Word goes a lot further than offering conventional keyboard commands, however. For instance, though not all menu items list alternative keyboard commands, you can still choose any menu command through the keyboard. You can also even make up your own keyboard commands.

Choosing menu commands. To choose any menu command with the keyboard, first hit Command-Tab (hold down the Command key, and press Tab simultaneously), and *Word's* menu bar will become highlighted. Now type a number from 0 to 8 to pull down *Word's* corresponding menu (0 being the Apple menu, 1 being the File menu, 2 being Edit, etc.). While the menu bar is highlighted, you can also use the left and right arrow keys to move through the various menus. With a menu pulled down, type the first letter of the command you'd like to use, and *Word* highlights the first command starting with that letter. If your desired command is below the selected command, type the first letter again, and *Word* moves to the next command beginning with that letter. Using the mouse may initially seem more expedient than this approach, but take my word that using the keyboard to select commands can quickly become second nature.

Choosing dialog box commands. You can also use the keyboard to choose dialog box buttons and options. Hit Command-Tab (or the Decimal key on the numeric

keypad) to move from one dialog box item to the next—
Word indicates the current item by placing a blinking
underline beneath it. To select the current blinking
item, hit Command-Space Bar (or 0 on the keypad).

You can also select many dialog box options by hitting
Command and the first letter of the option. For instance,
if I wanted to select the Manual Feed option from the
Print dialog box, I'd hit Command-M (making sure I'm
in the appropriate dialog box first).

Making your own keyboard commands. Through the
Commands feature (under the Tools menu), you can
actually define and redefine keyboard shortcuts for any
Word function. See page 210 for details.

GETTING ONLINE HELP

I've tried to explain all the important things you need to
know about *Word* 5.0 in this book, but you won't hurt my
feelings if you look for help from a different source.
Word itself includes a considerable online help dictionary, which you can use by choosing About Microsoft
Word from the Apple menu, and then clicking the Help
button. *Word* opens its Help dialog box, and lists an
assortment of topics you can learn more about. Select a
topic, and click the Help button (or double-click the

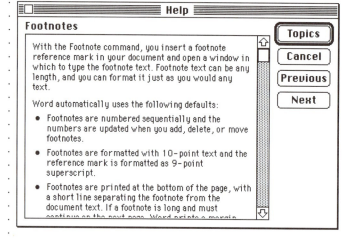

From the Apple menu, choose About Microsoft Word, and then click the Help button to use Word's Online Help system. Here Word explains its Footnote feature.

topic). *Word* responds with a rundown of that feature. You can use the Next and Previous buttons to move on to other topics on the list you just picked from.

Getting specific help. Sometimes it's tedious to track down specific information with the approach above. If you need help about a specific menu command, or even an option listed in a dialog box, then take these steps. From within *Word's* normal document window (not within the Help dialog box), press Command-?, and your mouse pointer becomes a large question mark. Now select a menu item or dialog box option, and *Word* opens its Help box with specific information on the command you've just picked.

To get feature-specific help, hit Command-?, and Word's mouse pointer becomes a question mark symbol. Then click the menu item or dialog box option you'd like help with.

Note: If you want to cancel the question mark pointer before choosing a command, just hit the Escape key.

System 7 Balloon Help. If your Mac is running Apple's System 7, then *Word* can also provide advice through Balloon Help. To turn this feature on, choose Show Balloons from the Help menu (the Help menu sits under the ballooned question mark icon to the right of *Word's* menu bar). When you move your mouse pointer to almost any *Word* button, icon, or other element, watch for pop-up help balloons that offer explanations in brief.

If you have System 7, click this icon to toggle Balloon Help on and off.

After a short while, however, you'll probably find *Word's* Balloon Help tedious. To turn it off, just choose Hide Balloons from the Help menu.

CHAPTER 2

Formatting Text

What's Inside

- Word's Ruler and Ribbon
- Setting Margin Indents and Tabs
- The Character Command
- The Paragraph Command
- Numbering Lines and Paragraphs
- Styles and the Style Sheet
- Making Tables

CHAPTER TWO ▾ Formatting Text

Formatting text in *Word* means a lot more than choosing a good-looking font. Your main formatting tools consist of *Word's* Character and Paragraph commands—Character handles type specifications, like font, style, point size, and color, while Paragraph's domain is margins, indentation, tab settings, line spacing and more. Two other tools you'll use regularly are *Word's* Ruler and Ribbon, which turn text formatting into a few quick and simple mouse clicks. *Word's* Style Sheet automates formatting and reformatting text, and is probably the most important feature you'll find in the program—definitely spend a few minutes getting acquainted with it. Finally, the Table feature takes much of the tedium out of turning raw text into good-looking, easily manageable tables.

WORD'S RULER AND RIBBON

Much of the text formatting that you'll want to do can be accomplished with *Word's* Ruler and the new Ribbon—both of these sit at the top of your document window, and give quick access to common formatting functions, without calling up complex dialog boxes and other command windows. Although the two work similarly, the Ruler affects various paragraph settings, such as text alignment, line spacing, tab marks, and more. The Ribbon, on the other hand, is used for setting font, point size, and styles like Bold and Italic, and has some other features besides. Both items can be turned on and off independently.

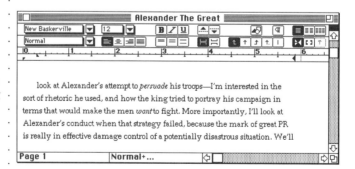

This document window displays both the Ruler and Ribbon at the same time. Keeping these two tools turned on can make formatting text quick and convenient.

The Ribbon

Choose Ribbon from *Word's* View menu, or hit Command-Option-R, to toggle *Word's* Ribbon on and off. As you work in your document, you can highlight text, and then make selections on the Ribbon to format it. Or, without highlighting anything, simply make your formatting selections and *Word* will apply them to everything you type thereafter—that is, until you change formatting again.

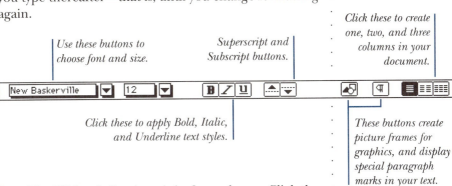

Use these buttons to choose font and size.

Superscript and Subscript buttons.

Click these to create one, two, and three columns in your document.

Click these to apply Bold, Italic, and Underline text styles.

These buttons create picture frames for graphics, and display special paragraph marks in your text.

Font. The Ribbon's first item is its font selector. Click the downwards arrow to see all the fonts installed in your Mac, and make your selection. You can also click and highlight the font name bar on the left, and type in the first few letters of the font you'd like, and hit Return.

Size. Click and highlight the size bar, type in your desired point size (from 4 to 16383), and then hit Return. Use the downwards arrow to see which point sizes of a particular font have been installed in your Mac. If you recall, the Mac uses "screen fonts" to display type on-screen. These come in predetermined sizes, such as 10, 12, and 24 points, where such specific sizes have been specially designed to look their best on screen, and print best with certain printers such as the ImageWriter (this is only the case if you're *not* using a font enhancing utility like *Adobe Type Manager*, or the TrueType technology in Apple's System 7 software. If you are using these items, your Mac automatically displays and prints any point size beautifully).

Style buttons. Click the Bold, Italic, and Underline buttons to apply those font styles to text. These buttons will become highlighted when on—click again to turn

CHAPTER TWO ▾ Formatting Text

the style formatting off. Likewise, use the Up and Down arrow buttons to Superscript, and Subscript, respectively, your text selections. To adjust the space that offsets the Superscript and Subscript, use the Character command (see page 53).

Picture button. Click this to insert a graphic frame at the point of your text cursor. See page 102, chapter five, for more details about creating graphics and frames.

Paragraph button. Click this to toggle *Word's* Show ¶ feature on and off. When this button is highlighted, *Word* displays dots between word spaces, and paragraph marks at the end of paragraphs, to help you visualize the document's formatting. More on this on page 55.

Column buttons. Click these to set type in one, two, and three columns respectively. The column setting you choose will affect all of your text, not just a selected passage. You can, however, break a document into sections, each of which can have its own distinct column formatting. See page 72 for more about sections and columns.

The Ruler

Choose Ruler from the View menu, or press Command-R, to toggle *Word's* Ruler on and off. Highlight text, and then choose the appropriate settings on the Ruler to format the selection. Or, without highlighting anything, simply make your formatting selections and *Word* applies

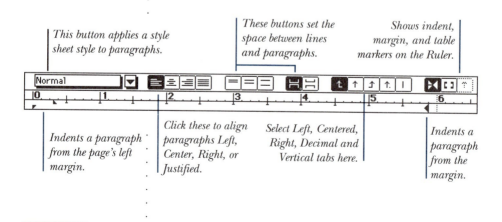

This button applies a style sheet style to paragraphs.

These buttons set the space between lines and paragraphs.

Shows indent, margin, and table markers on the Ruler.

Indents a paragraph from the page's left margin.

Click these to align paragraphs Left, Center, Right, or Justified.

Select Left, Centered, Right, Decimal and Vertical tabs here.

Indents a paragraph from the margin.

them to everything you type thereafter—until you make another change. Note that the Ruler's formatting only applies to whole paragraphs—for instance, you can't set line spacing so that the first two lines of a paragraph are double spaced, while the rest are single. *Word* insists that the entire paragraph be either single or double spaced, and this goes for all the other Ruler functions.

Margin indent ruler. Use the bottom part of *Word's* Ruler—the actual ruler part—to set the margin indents and tabs for your paragraphs. Notice the Left and Right indent indicators on either side—you can drag these with the mouse to indent paragraphs from the margins of your page (these margins are set with the Document command—page 74). Setting tabs is a matter of clicking a tab marker at the appropriate place on the Ruler. See *Setting Margin Indents and Tabs* on page 50 for details.

Style button. The Ruler's left-most button lets you select styles from your style sheet. We haven't talked about styles yet, but will soon (page 61 if you can't wait). Click the downwards arrow to see all the styles for your document, and make your selection. You can also click and highlight the style name bar itself, type the first few letters of the style you'd like, and then hit Return.

Text alignment. Click these to align a paragraph to the left, right, or center of your page, or to justify both left and right margins.

Line and paragraph spacing. Click to specify single, double, or triple spacing, respectively. Occasionally, none will be suitable, so use the Paragraph command under Format (page 56) to set your own custom line spacing. Likewise, the paragraph spacing icons apply extra white space to the tops of paragraphs—you can choose between no space, and space (about 12 points), respectively. You can also create custom paragraph spacing with the Paragraph command. See page 56.

Tabs markers. Click these to select left-aligning, centered-aligning, right-aligning, decimal point-aligning and vertical tabs marks for the Ruler. Then click anywhere on the Ruler to set the tab—you can also reposition the tab

Much of the formatting you set from the Ruler affects an entire paragraph, rather than selected parts. Either highlight the paragraph (or paragraphs), or place Word's text cursor in the paragraph you'd like to affect. Then use the Ruler to apply formatting.

The Ruler usually measures by inches, but you can set it to display centimeters, points, or picas. Choose Preferences from the Tools menu.

by dragging with the mouse, or delete it by dragging it off the Ruler. See the next section for more tab details.

Indent, margin and table markers. Use the last three buttons on the right side of the Ruler to display either indent markers, margin markers or table markers on your Ruler. You're already familiar with indent markers—they're the little arrow-icons that sit on the Ruler and let you indent a paragraph in from its page margin. Likewise, click the margin marker button to see and set your page margins on the Ruler. Remember that whatever margins you set will affect your entire document, not just a selected paragraph or current page. Finally, the table marker button is handy for when you're designing tables—click it and the Ruler displays markers to indicate the position and width of columns in your table. You can drag the table markers along to Ruler to easily resize columns.

When you're simply editing text, however, you'll want to keep the indent marker button turned on, and only use the margin and table markers when they're actually called for.

SETTING MARGIN INDENTS AND TABS

You can set margin indents for paragraphs via *Word's* Ruler command—once again, by the way, a margin indent is the space that separates the paragraph from the page's margins (see page 74 about margins). Note that you can vary these indents from paragraph to paragraph, and that they are *in addition to* the overall, universal document margins that are set with the Document command. If you've set 1 inch left and right page margins in Document, then you'll increase that when you adjust your paragraph margins.

To set the left and right indents, simply click and drag the left and right indent markers on either side of the Ruler—this affects the particular paragraph that's currently highlighted, or that contains your text cursor.

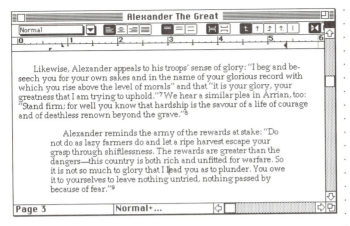

You can indent any paragraph by dragging its corresponding indent markers on Word's Ruler. Here I've formatted two paragraphs with different margin indents. The Ruler indicates the indents for the bottom paragraph.

Notice how the left indent marker is split in two, and that the two halves can be moved independently. Use the bottom half to set your paragraph's left indent, and the top to set an additional automatic indent for the first line of each paragraph.

Special indents. You can create some unique indents with Word. To make a "hanging indent," drag the bottom half of the left margin marker to the *right*, which sets an inset left margin. Then separately drag its top half further to the *left*. A "nested indent" is where you simply indent a paragraph further and further from the left margin. To quickly to do this, press Command-Shift-N. Try it out!

You can split the Ruler's left indent marker to further indent the first line of a paragraph.

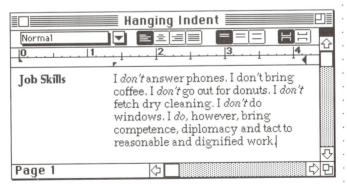

Here's a hanging indent for you. Notice how the first line "hangs" over the rest of the paragraph, and how the Ruler's left indent marker is split to accomplish this.

CHAPTER TWO ▼ Formatting Text

Setting Tabs

Setting tabs in your paragraphs is not complicated. First, select the desired tab type from the Ruler—as I've said, you can pick left, centered, right, decimal or vertical tabs. Click anywhere on the Ruler to set a tab in the selected paragraph or paragraphs (which are either highlighted, or contains the text cursor)—set as many as you like across the Ruler. When typing in a paragraph you've applied tabs to, simply hit the Tab key to jump from one tab to the next. Note: you may want to set tabs more precisely than the Ruler will allow, or you may want to create leaders, such as dots or lines that fill in tabbed space. Use *Word's* Paragraph feature—see page 57.

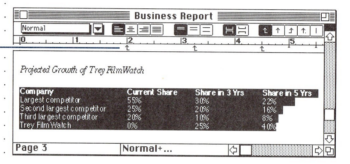

Notice how Word's Ruler shows the tab markers for this highlighted table. You could resize the table's columns by dragging the appropriate tab markers on the Ruler.

Current Share
55%
25%
20%
0%

Center-tabbed text is centered at the tab's position.

Current Share
55%
25%
20%
0%

Right-tabbed text aligns right to the tab's position.

Current Share
55.53%
25.3%
20.85%
0.0%

Decimal-tabbed text aligns by the decimal point's position.

Current Share
55%
25%
20%
0%

Vertical tabs print a vertical line in the tab's position.

Moving and removing tabs. You can move tabs by dragging their markers to a new location on the Ruler. If you've already tabbed text in your paragraph, *Word* will automatically shift the text to reflect its tab's new location. To delete a tab, just drag its marker off the Ruler, and release the mouse button. Any text set to the removed tab shifts to the next tab on the right. And remember, if you're moving or removing a tab that you applied to a group of paragraphs, be sure to highlight the paragraphs first.

When to use tabs, and when not to. Sometimes tabs are the most convenient way to set columns in a paragraph—for instance, they're convenient for creating a resume, or a simple table such as a calendar of events. But many people use tabs to create involved tables of data, and consequently waste considerable time inserting, removing, and adjusting one tab after another. If you're creating tables, consider *Word's* convenient Table feature. See page 64.

You can't change a tab's orientation once it's been set on the Ruler—for instance, change a left tab to a centered tab. You'll have to remove the old tab, and then insert a new one in the same place.

THE CHARACTER COMMAND

You'll use Character to define the look of your text—its font, point size, style, such as Bold or Italic, and a host of other attributes.

How to use Character. You can take two approaches to formatting text with Character—first is to highlight existing text with your mouse, and then choose Character from the Format menu (or hit Command-D), and apply your formatting to that particular text selection. The alternative is to simply choose Character with no text selected—whatever formatting you choose then applies to everything you type thereafter, until you again change the formatting.

Setting Character Attributes

With the Character box called up, you simply pick your desired text attributes. The Font button lists all the fonts installed in your Mac. In Size, you can type in a value measured by points, in the range of 4 to 16383 points—plenty for all occasions. Click the downwards arrow to see

Chapter Two ▼ Formatting Text

Choosing Character from the Format menu (or pressing Command-D) gives you Word's Character box. From here, you can set a variety of formatting for text.

By the way, if you highlight text, and then choose Character, some of these style check boxes may appear gray. That means that your highlighted text includes both on and off cases of a particular style. For instance, a gray Italic box means that there's both Italic and non-Italic text in the selection.

You can set font and size formatting from the keyboard. Press Command-Shift-E, type in the first few letters of a font's name and hit Return. Likewise, use Command-Shift and the > and < keys to increase and decrease a font's size.

which point sizes of a particular font have been installed in your Mac. If you recall, the Mac uses presized "screen fonts" to display type on-screen. These come in predetermined sizes, such as 10, 12, and 24 points, so the characters look their best on screen. You can, of course, select *any* point size, but the prebuilt screen font sizes will always look best on-screen, and print best with certain printers such as the ImageWriter or StyleWriter (this is only the case if you're *not* using a font enhancing utility like *Adobe Type Manager,* or the TrueType technology in Apple's System 7 software. If you are using these items, your Mac automatically displays and prints any point size beautifully).

As you might have guessed, Underline lets you pick a number of underline styles (single, double, dotted, etc.), while Color gives you a choice of eight predetermined colors to apply to type. In the Position box, the Superscript and Subscript options let you set a characters above or below the standard text baseline, respectively—type in the number of points to shift the text by. Likewise, Spacing lets you Expand or Condense letters—just enter the desired point value.

54

Finally, use Style to specify **Bold**, *Italic*, Outline, Shadow, S̶t̶r̶i̶k̶e̶t̶h̶r̶u̶, SMALL CAPS (ALL LETTERS IN CAPITALS, ALTHOUGH THE INITIAL CAPS ARE LARGEST), ALL CAPS, or Hidden text styles.

The Hidden Style. Hidden style text won't print in your document, and only shows on screen if the option is selected by *Word's* Preferences feature (you'll know text is Hidden by a dotted underline). You might use this style to write notes and commentary in a manuscript, knowing they'll appear to you on screen, but won't clutter the final printed document. Just remember that Hidden text can create discrepancies in the line endings and even page breaks in your document, since *Word* accounts for it when paginating on-screen, but doesn't account for it when paginating for the printer. To see your document on-screen exactly as it appears on paper, make sure to uncheck the Show Hidden Text option in the View section of *Word's* Preferences command.

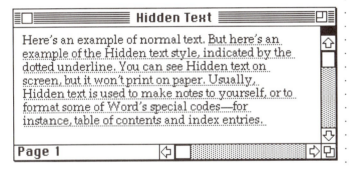

Hidden text won't print on paper, but it does appear on-screen—here's what it looks like.

Apply button. If you've highlighted text, clicking Apply formats the selection with whatever character attributes you've selected, but won't close the Character box—you're free to select attributes again. It's a convenient way of previewing and experimenting with text attributes without opening and closing Character each time.

THE PARAGRAPH COMMAND

Word's Paragraph feature gives you control over how the paragraphs in your document are formatted—how much

The spacing area lets you set the white space that appears before and after a paragraph, as well as the space between text lines of a paragraph.

Type in values to set a paragraph's indentation from the page's margin.

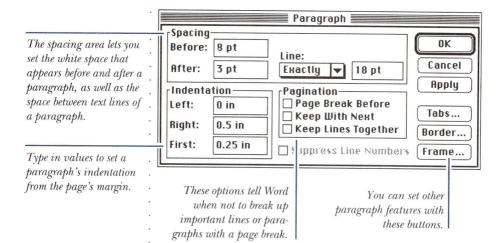

These options tell Word when not to break up important lines or paragraphs with a page break.

You can set other paragraph features with these buttons.

space comes before and after paragraphs, how much space sits between text lines, what sort of tab settings are used, and more. Many of this command's features are also offer by the Ruler, but Paragraph lets you make some finer adjustments to formatting. Remember that *Word* applies your formatting either to a selected paragraph (or paragraphs), or to the one that contains your text cursor. In any case, choose Paragraph from the Format menu (or hit Command-M)—*Word* produces the appropriate dialog box, and also puts its Ruler at the top of your document.

Paragraph and line spacing. Here you can type in how much space, in points, for *Word* to put before and after the paragraph. You can also specify the paragraph's exact line spacing, in points rather than by single-, double-, and triple-spacing measurements. The Auto spacing option simply uses single spacing as the standard default. If you want custom line spacing, click the downwards arrow and select either At Least or Exactly. Then type in your custom spacing. Choosing At Least tells *Word* that it can even add a little more line spacing to a paragraph, so it can fit a paragraph or certain lines of a paragraph on the same page (I'll talk about this option in a moment). Choosing Exactly, on the other hand, doesn't give it this flexibility for improvisation.

Margin indents. Left and Right values refer to your left and right margin indents. You can type in margin settings here, or click and drag the indent indicators on the Ruler—notice how the value boxes automatically reflect the measurements you're setting. If you want your paragraph to start with an automatic first line indent, then type the indent's measurement into the First value box. You can also set the value by dragging the top part of the split left margin marker on the Ruler.

Pagination. *Word's* Pagination options let you decide whether paragraphs will be split by page breaks. Basically, you highlight a particular paragraph (or place the cursor in it), and then choose one of the Pagination options. *Page Break Before* means that *Word* will always start a new page for each paragraph that has this option checked. *Keep With Next* will insure that the paragraph, and the one immediately following it, will print on the same page, and won't be divided by a page break (unless the two won't fit on a single page). In doing this, *Word* may have to stop printing text midway on the previous page, so it can start the *Keep With Next* paragraphs on a new page, where they'll fit together. Likewise, *Keep Lines Together* will stop an important paragraph from being divided by a page break.

Other buttons. Use the Tabs button to set tabs, without clicking them on the Ruler. Click the type of tab you'd like, and then type in its location in the Position box. Click Set to actually place it. Likewise, Clear removes the tab, and Clear All removes all tabs you've set. You may also want to choose an appropriate Leader, such as dots or dashes, to fill in tabbed space. Click Border if you want to add some highlighting graphics to your paragraph, such as a frame, or background gray screen. I explain Border in chapter five, page 111. The Frame button lets you position paragraphs separately from the rest of your text, anywhere on the page. It's a powerful feature that gives *Word* some of the flexibility of a page layout program, and I explain it on page 148. Finally, clicking Apply gives you a preview of whatever formatting you've set for your paragraphs. Click OK when you're happy with the results.

Numbering Lines and Paragraphs

If your documents require numbered lines and paragraphs—for instance, in legal contracts, or technical manuals, scripts, or even *poetry*—then *Word* has what you need.

Numbering Lines

Numbering the lines in your document is easy. First select the text you'd like to number—if it's the entire document, you can skip this step. Then choose Section from the Format menu, and click the Line Numbers button in that dialog box.

From the Line Numbers box, you'll have a few simple choices to make. First is to decide if you want line numbers to restart at 1 on every new page, every new section (these are the sections you might have created earlier with *Word's* Section feature—page 72), or whether the numbers should run continuously throughout your entire document. Click the Line Numbers button to make your selection. In the Count By box, you can specify the increment in which line numbers should appear in your document. A "1" means that *Word* prints a number next to every line in your text—this can become cluttered. In many cases, an increment of 5 is desirable.

You can set line numbering so that it restarts with every new page, section, or span continuously throughout a document.

Line number positions. Finally, *Word* prints line numbers in the page margin to the left of your text, with .25-inch space between the numbers and the margin of your text. To change the space between numbers and text, type in your own value into the From Text box.

Viewing line numbers. Curiously, *Word* doesn't display the line numbers you set in either its Normal or Page Layout view. To see the numbers and their positioning, choose Print Preview from the File menu.

Numbering Paragraphs

To number paragraphs, first select the desired paragraphs—if the entire document, there's no need to select anything. Then choose Renumber from the Tools menu to call up the appropriate dialog box. In the Start At box, type in the number you'd like the paragraphs to count from. And in the Format box, you can type in a number format, more like a style, that *Word* should use in numbering your paragraphs. For Arabic numerals (1, 2, 3...), type "1". For Roman numerals (I, II, III...), type "I" for uppercase and "i" for lowercase. Likewise, use "A" and "a" for an alphabet format. You can also type these formats with brackets, parenthesis, periods, colons or other symbols to help distinguish the numbers from the document text they're applied to. For instance, typing "1)" into the Format box will number paragraphs as 1), 2), 3) etc. Typing "a." will allow a., b., c., and so on.

Numbering multilevel paragraphs. If your document is hierarchically organized by main headings, subheadings, and still further headings, *Word* can number each of these heading levels separately to help emphasize the hierarchy of the document. *Word's* Renumber feature automatically recognizes the various paragraph levels in your document by looking for different style sheet styles, heading styles from *Word's* Outline feature, or paragraph indents set with the Ruler (not by tabs or spaces).

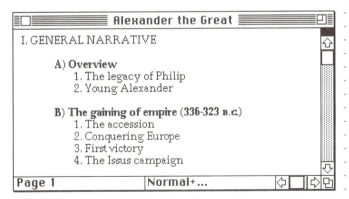

These paragraphs demonstrate Word's talent for numbering paragraphs. First level paragraphs are numbered I. II. III., second levels are A), B), C), and so on.

CHAPTER TWO ▾ Formatting Text

You can tell Word how to number multilevel paragraphs by entering instructions in the Format box. According to this example's Format box, Word will number first level paragraphs with roman numerals (I, II, III), second level paragraphs with uppercase alphabet letters, and third level paragraphs with familiar arabic numerals.

```
════════════ Renumber ════════════
Paragraphs:  ● All   ○ Only If Already Numbered
Start at: [1]           Format: [I.A.1]
Numbers:  ● 1   ○ 1.1...   ○ By Example   ○ Remove
   [  OK  ]   [ Cancel ]
```

You can number different paragraph levels by typing each level's unique number format into the Format box, separating each with a period (.). It sounds confusing, but take this example. Suppose your document has three paragraph levels. By typing "I.A.1.a.i", *Word* would number your paragraphs in a standard outline format—first level paragraphs (or headings) by roman numerals, (I, II, III), your second level by uppercase alphabet letters, and your third level by arabic numerals, and so on. You'll get the hang of this with a little trial and error.

You can also number your paragraph levels in a 1.1 format (1.1, 1.2, 2.1, 2.2, 2.3) by selecting the 1.1 option in the Renumber dialog box.

Numbering Paragraphs by Example

A quick way to set up a paragraph numbering scheme is to manually number the first instance of each paragraph level in your document. For instance, try manually typing "I)" at the beginning of a first level paragraph, and "A." at the beginning of a second level paragraph. Also remember to follow each manual entry by hitting the tab key to separate the paragraph number from its text. Then highlight those example paragraphs along with the rest of the text you want numbered, and choose Renumber from Tools. The By Example option should be turned on—click OK and *Word* numbers all your paragraphs according to your example.

💧 *To remove paragraph numbers, highlight the numbered text, choose Renumber from the Tools menu, and check the Remove option.*

Updating Paragraph Numbers

If you add, remove, or rearrange the numbered paragraphs in your document, you'll want to update the numbers to reflect these changes. First highlight the desired paragraphs—if the entire document, there's no need to highlight. Choose Renumber from the Tools menu, and click the By Example option so *Word* uses the same number format already set up in your document. Then click OK to renumber the paragraphs.

STYLES AND THE STYLE SHEET

The Style Sheet is one of *Word's* best features, but many people never use it. Don't join this crowd! *Word's* Style Sheet is important for two reasons: first, it lets you automate paragraph formatting. You create a "style" for every type of paragraph formatting in your document—for instance, you might create separate styles for headings, subheads, body text, and captions—and assign each style its particular formatting information, such as font, point size, line spacing, paragraph alignment, indentation and so on. Now, when you want to format paragraphs in your document, just choose the appropriate style—like Subhead or Body Copy—and *Word* automatically formats the text with that style's attributes. The second advantage to styles is that if you decide to change existing formatting in a document—make subheads bigger, for instance—then just update the appropriate style and *Word* applies your change to all the paragraphs previously formatted in that style.

The Style Sheet is simply the collection of all styles used by a particular document. Each Word document can have its own unique style sheet (and therefore, its own unique styles).

Creating a Style

Choose Style from the Format menu, or hit Command-T, to call up the Style dialog box. Type a style name into the Style box. Now use the Font menu, the Character and Paragraph commands, and Ruler and Ribbon (if you've turned them on) to choose the attributes for your style—*Word* will let you access these features even though the Style dialog box is open. By the way, notice how *Word* lists each attribute under the Style name. Now click the Define button to add your new style to the style sheet.

Basing one style on another. Sometimes you'll create a style that is very similar to an existing one, except for one or two attributes—perhaps point size, or bold formatting, for instance. To avoid resetting all the attributes again, type or select from the menu the original style name into

CHAPTER TWO ▼ Formatting Text

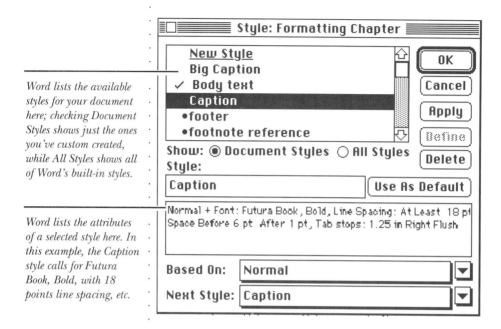

Word lists the available styles for your document here; checking Document Styles shows just the ones you've custom created, while All Styles shows all of Word's built-in styles.

Word lists the attributes of a selected style here. In this example, the Caption style calls for Futura Book, Bold, with 18 points line spacing, etc.

❗ *Word tells you the style of the current paragraph at the bottom of your document window. You can quickly call up Word's Style dialog box by double-clicking this region.*

❗ *You can quickly apply styles with the keyboard. Hit Command-Shift-S, type in the first few characters of the style's name, and hit Return.*

the Based On box, and the new style you're creating will take on its attributes.

Next Style. You can set *Word* to follow one paragraph style with a different style in the next paragraph you type—for instance, to follow a headline with a subhead. Choose the follow-up style's name here.

Applying a Style

First, highlight a passage, or place the text cursor in the paragraph you'd like to format. Choose Style from the Format menu (or Command-T) and select the style to apply. Click Apply to see a preview of your formatted text, or OK to return to the document. Your text will be formatted with the style's attributes.

You can also apply styles using *Word's* Ruler, if it's turned on. With a passage or single paragraph selected, click and hold the Ruler's left-most Style button to choose the desired style.

Modifying a Style

Choose Style from the Format menu (or Command-T) and select the style to modify. Now, as if you were creating it from scratch, use the Font menu, Character and Paragraph commands, and Ruler and Ribbon (if turned on) to modify that style's existing attributes—then click Define to finalize the change. When you return to your document, *Word* automatically updates all the text formatted in the style to reflect your changes.

Another quick way to modify a style is to change the formatting of some text in that style (as you would normally, by highlighting the text and then applying character and paragraph formatting). Place your text cursor in that changed text, and then use the Ruler's Style button to choose the same style you've just modified. *Word* asks if you want to reapply the style to the selected text, or redefine it based on the new text. Pick the latter.

> 💡 *Word uses the Normal style to format text in new documents, so modify Normal with whatever attributes you like. Or you can create your own style, and use the Style box's Use As Default button to make it Word's standard, default style.*

```
Style: Body text                              [ OK ]
  ⦿ Reapply the style to the selection?      [Cancel]
  ○ Redefine the style based on selection?
```

> *You'll see this dialog box when trying to redefine a style based on a text selection in your document. Choose the latter option.*

More About Styles

Each document you create has its own Style Sheet—that is, its own unique collection of styles. So you don't have to create the same styles from scratch with every new document, *Word* lets you copy a Style Sheet from one document to another. Open the Style box, and then choose Open from the File menu. Select the document with the desired style sheet, and *Word* copies its styles into your new document.

In the Style box, if the Document Styles button is on, *Word* only displays the styles that you've created. There are actually more prebuilt styles in your document, which *Word* uses for all sorts of occasions—for instance, to format your index, table of contents, footnotes, page numbers, outline headings, and more. *Word* doesn't usually display these unless there's a need to—for instance, if you're actually using footnotes, or creating an index that calls for those styles. To see *all* the styles in your document, however, just click the All Styles button.

> 💡 *If you've manually added additional formatting to text in a certain style (either with the Ruler, Ribbon, or other formatting features) you can highlight the text, and choose Revert to Style (from the Format menu) to remove that extra formatting, and bring the text back to its original, unmodified style.*

Making Tables

Word takes much of the tedium out of creating data tables in your documents. Ordinarily, you might be tempted to make tables with tabs—*don't*. The Table feature lets you build your tables on a flexible, dynamic grid, which you can quickly set up and adjust. For instance, adding, deleting, or resizing columns and rows is accomplished with a few menu selections or drags of the mouse. *Word* also enhances tables with graphical borders and shading so they look good, too.

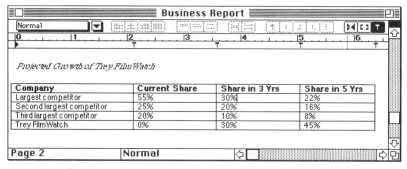

Here's a fairly simple, straightforward table—just four columns by five rows.

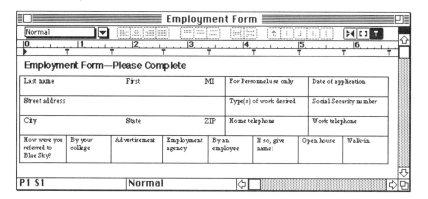

This table is more advanced, with cells of varying sizes, and multiple text lines in single cells.

Creating a Table

Position your text cursor where a new table should appear, and choose Table from the Insert menu to bring up the appropriate dialog box. Now type in the desired number of columns and rows, along with the width for each column. Hit OK and *Word* places your custom table in the document—notice the cell grid is indicated by a gray outline. Before hitting OK, you can also click the Format button to specify some other parameters, especially pertaining to the Rows of text in your table. This brings you to the Table Cells command, which I'll talk about below in *Modifying a Table*.

Keep Word's Ruler and Ribbon turned on—they make working with tables easier.

Choosing Table from the Insert menu lets you define a new table in terms of columns and rows.

Convert existing text into tables. You can create tables from existing data in your documents, such as text separated by tabs or commas (perhaps you imported this information from a spreadsheet or database). Highlight the text to convert, and then choose Text to Table under the Insert menu. In the Convert To area, specify the text format you're trying to convert (*Word* may have already guessed). You can select tab and comma "delimited" text so that *Word* puts text separated by a tab or comma into a table cell. If you select a series of paragraphs, *Word* puts each paragraph in its own single-celled table row. Side by Side Paragraphs will each be placed in cells of the same row (side by side paragraphs, however, are from the *Word* 3.0 days—you'll probably never use them now).

Chapter Two ▾ Formatting Text

Entering and Formatting Data

To enter text into your table, just position your cursor in a table cell and type in its data. You can type multiple lines into a cell, and *Word* automatically increases the height of its row to accommodate the text. To move to the next column, hit either Tab or the right arrow key. Likewise, use the left arrow to move backwards a column, and up and down arrows to move across rows.

Formatting data. *Word* formats each cell as if it were a separate paragraph, so you can set Ruler margins, text alignment (left, center, right) and other paragraph attributes for each. You can also set font, point size, style, and other character attributes as well. The procedure works just as if you were formatting regular text—click the cursor in a cell, or highlight a range of cells, and then use the Ruler to adjust cell margins, or change fonts, or what have you.

By the way, all of *Word's* familiar editing features such as Cut, Copy, Paste, and Clear work with table data. You can, for instance, cut and paste one column's data to a new column.

❗ *Word formats the text in your table according to the style sheet style of the paragraph you inserted the table into. This may be the Normal style, or a custom style you created. Neither may be very suitable for tables, however—for instance, paragraph indentation or margins could be odd looking. The solution is to create a custom table style, and then apply it to the table.*

Make sure this symbol is highlighted before using the Ruler to format text in a table.

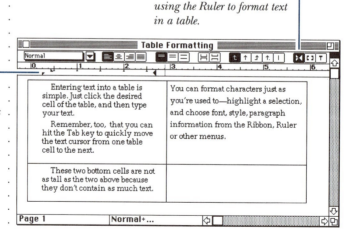

Notice how the Ruler displays the margin indents for the text in this particular table cell. You can use the Ruler to apply all sorts of formatting to table text.

66

Modifying a Table

You can easily change the design of an existing table—for instance, by adding, removing, or resizing columns and rows. *Word* automatically adjusts the table to reflect your alterations.

Resizing columns. To easily resize columns, first turn on *Word's* Ruler (under the View menu), and select the column to resize. Now click the right-most icon on the Ruler (it looks like a capital T—you won't be able to choose it if you haven't already selected a column). Notice how *Word's* Ruler now places a T mark to indicate the boundaries of the corresponding columns. Simply drag the ruler T marks to resize the particular column. Notice how *Word* automatically shifts the other columns to account for the adjusted size.

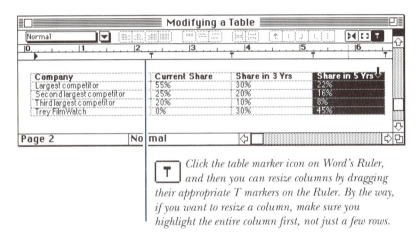

Click the table marker icon on *Word's* Ruler, and then you can resize columns by dragging their appropriate T markers on the Ruler. By the way, if you want to resize a column, make sure you highlight the entire column first, not just a few rows.

Adding and deleting rows and columns. These functions are carried out by choosing Table Layout from the Format menu. Removing rows and columns is easy—first select the unwanted elements (you can select a single column, row or a range), choose Table Layout and click the Delete button. To add, first highlight the column or row that should come *after* your new addition. Then choose Table Layout and click the Insert button. If you want to add multiple rows or columns, then highlight a range of existing ones. *Word* adds as many columns or rows highlighted when you issue the Insert command.

> To delete an entire table, highlight the table and an empty line above or below it—then hit Delete or Backspace. You can also use the Table Layout feature (under Format) to delete tables.

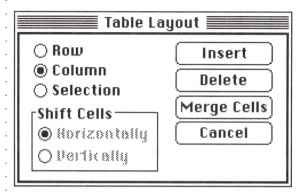

Word's Table Layout feature (under the Format menu) lets you insert, delete, and merge table cells, columns, and rows. Before choosing Table Layout, be sure to highlight the part of the table you'd like to affect.

A word of advice: Be sure to select an entire row or column, rather than just a cell, before using Insert or Delete. Otherwise, *Word* just affects an individual cell, which can throw your table design off.

Merging cells. To merge multiple cells into one large cell—for instance to make a header extending across the table—highlight the cells, choose Table Layout from Format, and click the Merge Cells button. Take the same steps, but click the Split Cell button, to reverse a merge.

Other modifications. You can make other changes by choosing Table Cells under the Format menu. Ordinarily, *Word* uses Auto Row Height, which sizes a row according to the size of text and lines it holds. But you can type in a custom height in points for selected rows. The Exact option means that *Word* cuts off any material higher than your custom row height. At Least means it adjusts the row height to accommodate even higher material. Space Between Columns refers to the measure of space separating text in side by side columns, not the columns themselves. Indent lets you indent selected rows on the page by a specified measurement. You can also do this by highlighting rows, and moving their left margins with *Word's* Ruler. And Alignment lets you align selected rows Left, Center, or Right on the page.

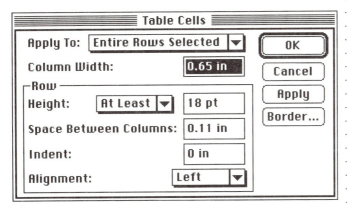

The Table Cells box (under the Format menu) lets you control some aspects of a table's text, such as margin indents in table cells, and text alignment (left, right, centered, etc.).

Adding Visual Polish to Tables

Word displays new tables with dotted grid lines that display on-screen, but don't print on paper. Consequently, you'll probably want to customize the look of your tables. *Word* offers a number of options, allowing you to frame tables, or even single cells, with a variety of borders. You can also add gray-shaded backgrounds to tables, or just to specific cells, rows, or columns to highlight important information.

The Border command. All of this is done through *Word's* Border feature, which I explain fully on page 111. You can set up a table's look as soon you create it with the Table command under the Insert menu.

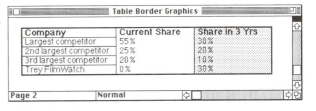

The table in this window may not be pretty, but it nonetheless demonstrates the graphic borders and gray shading you can apply to tables.

After specifying the table's numbers of columns and rows, hit the Format button and then, at the next dialog box, the Border button. Here you'll define how to frame the table and its cells. For existing tables, you can simply highlight cells, columns, rows, or your entire table, and then choose Border from the Format menu.

Applying graphics is a matter of telling *Word* which sides of particular cells, or the entire table, to place a border on (left, right, top, bottom), and which type of line style to use (single, thick, double lines, etc.). You might also apply a gray shade to your selection. Again, see page 115 for more details.

CHAPTER 3

Setting Up a Document

What's Inside

- Sections in a Document
- Setting Page Size, Orientation, and Margins
- Setting Up Columns
- Page Numbers
- Headers and Footers

When designing a document, there are issues to consider other than the best looking font. For instance, you might want to establish custom page margins, or set multiple columns, add headers and footers, page numbers, and more—all of which I'll explain here. Before anything else, however, I'll look at *Word's* Section command, which gives you a great deal of flexibility in designing documents. Ordinarily, *Word* applies many of its features—columns, headers/footers, page number styles, and much more—throughout your entire document. That's bad news in many cases. For instance, you might want to vary column settings from page to page in the same document, or apply different headers and footers to different chapters in the same document. Fortunately, *Word's* Section feature overcomes this limitation.

SECTIONS IN A DOCUMENT

Word's Section feature lets you break your document into multiple parts, where each part can have a different collection of settings. For instance, you can use sections to divide a document into multiple chapters, each with different headers or footers and page numbering schemes. Or suppose you're designing a newsletter that called for a three-column layout, with a masthead extending across the page. You'd create a section for the single-column masthead, and then a new section right below it for the three columns of text.

Creating Sections

Position your text cursor at the point you'd like a new section to begin—even in a line of text. Then choose Section Break from the Insert menu, and *Word* places a section marker line directly below the cursor (if you position the cursor at the beginning of a paragraph, *Word* puts the section marker one line above). The new section begins directly below this marker, and continues to either the end of your document, or until another section is started.

By the way, if you're working in *Word's* Page Layout view, you won't see the section marker unless *Word's* Show ¶ feature is turned on (under the View menu).

Section numbering. *Word* numbers the sections in your document, calling the first section 1, and then counting sequentially from there. You can figure out which section you're currently in by checking the lower left corner of your document window. *Word* uses a format of *P1 S2*, where *P* refers to the page in the document or section, and *S* refers to the section.

Deleting a section. Use the text cursor to backspace over, or highlight and delete, the section line that begins the section you'd like to remove. The text and graphics in the doomed section aren't affected, except that they'll take on the formatting of the section below—column settings, headers and footers, page numbering, and all.

Applying Section Formatting

You can format a section in a number of ways, but the chief approach is by choosing Section from the Format menu. The Section dialog box lets you apply a number of settings that I talk about later on in this chapter, such as columns, page numbers, and header and footer positioning. What you should know here, however, is that you can specify how *Word* should print a new section. Sometimes you'll want a section to print on a new page—for instance, if the section marks the start of a new chapter. Or you might want the section to start immediately where the last one left off, in case you're creating a newsletter masthead directly above some text columns. To state your preference, click the Start button in the Section dialog box. You can set a different start, by the way, for each section in your document.

Notice that Word calls called Untitled*x (1, 2, 3, pp for details about savi*

The lower left corner of your document window tells you what page and section you're in.

💧 *When printing, Word assumes it should print all sections. You can, however, specify a range (section 1, page 1 to section 2, page 5) with the Print box's Section and Page From and To boxes.*

The Section dialog box lets you define a number of settings for the current section, from header/footer positioning to page number styles to column formats.

73

Setting Page Size, Orientation, and Margins

When you start a new document, *Word* formats it at the standard letter size of 8.5 by 11 inches. To use a different size, choose Page Setup under the File menu. If you're using a LaserWriter printer, you can pick between Legal (8.5 by 14 inches), A4 Letter (European standard, 21 by 29.7 cm.), B5 Letter (17.6 by 25 cm.), Tabloid (11 by 17 inches), and Standard US Business Envelope. ImageWriters can use US Letter, Legal, A4 Letter, International Fanfold (8.25 by 12 inches) and Computer Paper (14 by 11 inches).

Note: Your page size options can vary depending on the printer model you use. I address LaserWriter and ImageWriter printers here, but other models won't be much different.

Custom page sizes. To create a custom page size—for business cards or fliers, for instance—choose Preferences under the Tools menu. Type in your custom width and height dimensions into the appropriate value boxes, and then exit. Go back to the Page Setup box to select your custom measurements.

Page orientation. Ordinarily, *Word* prints your document in Portrait mode, so that the reader holds a page vertically to read. You can, however, print in Landscape mode, so *Word* prints your document horizontally across the wider dimension of the page. Pick your preference in the Page Setup box.

Use As Default. The page size and orientation you custom set applies only to the document you're currently working on. To have your settings apply to all new *Word* documents, check the Use As Default option.

Page Margins

The page margins you set in *Word* affect your whole document, and you can set them in a few ways. Most recommended is to choose Document from the Format menu, and then type in the Left, Right, Top, and Bottom margin values. *Word* will duplicate these exact margins on every page. If you're designing a document with

> 💡 *You can still print text and graphics in your pages' margins. Both left and right paragraph indents can extend into the margins, and you can use the Frame command (page 148) to place items in there, too.*

Setting Up a Document ▼ **CHAPTER THREE**

facing pages (where print appears on left and right side pages of bound documents), then check the Mirror Even/Odd option so left and right pages use Inside and Outside margins. Likewise, if your document will be bound, then add extra margin space for the binding by typing a value into the Gutter box (the "gutter" margin ensures that the binding doesn't cover up any text). Also notice the At Least buttons next to the top and bottom margin values—these tell you that *Word* may adjust your margins to accommodate any multiple-lined headers or footers you might have. If you don't want this adjustment, click the buttons and choose Exactly.

Page margins are constant, affecting every paragraph in your document. If you want to change the margins of select paragraphs, then indent them with Word's Ruler. These indents are added to the overall margin values.

Setting margins visually. There are two ways to set margins by eyeballing it. First is by choosing Print Preview from the File menu (or Command-Option-P) where horizontal and vertical margin boundary lines appear for the page you're previewing. Drag a boundary line's handle to readjust the margin (notice how *Word* displays the margin measurement at the top of the window as you drag). When you release the mouse, *Word* applies the new margin to your entire document. You can also set your horizontal page margins with *Word's* Ruler (under the View menu). Click the Margins icon on the Ruler's right side (the icon with the two facing brackets), and drag the left and right brackets across the Ruler to set the margins.

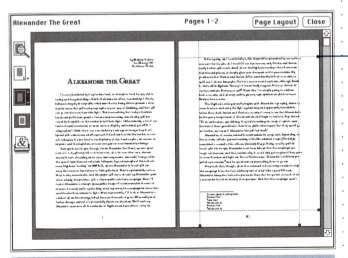

You can adjust page margins by dragging the page margin guides in Word's Print Preview (under the File menu).

75

Setting Up Columns

There are two recommended ways to set up multiple columns in *Word*. The quickest is to simply click the one- two- and three-column icons on the right hand side of *Word's* Ribbon, if it's turned on (check the View menu). Another option is to choose Section from the Format menu, and then type in your desired columns there. From the Section box, you can also specify the gutter space that separates each column. Either way, *Word* applies the columns to your entire document.

By the way, *Word* won't display columns side by side in its Normal view—it only formats text in a single strip at column size. To see side-by-side columns, you have to either work in Page Layout view (under the View menu), or choose Print Preview from File.

Resizing columns. One way to resize columns is to make sure you're in Page Layout view, call up *Word's* Ruler, and click the Margins icon on the Ruler's right side (the icon with the two facing brackets). *Word* places brackets on the Ruler to indicate column boundaries, which you can resize by dragging with the mouse. Unfortunately, you can't give columns different sizes.

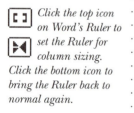
Click the top icon on Word's Ruler to set the Ruler for column sizing. Click the bottom icon to bring the Ruler back to normal again.

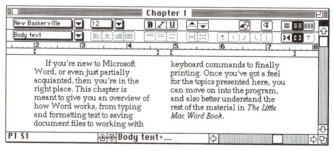

As an alternative to using the Ruler, you could also choose Section from the Format menu and type in a new value for the column's spacing.

Varying Columns in the Same Document

You'll probably not want a particular column format to apply to your *whole* document. For instance, if you're doing a newsletter, you might need three columns

Setting Up a Document ▼ CHAPTER THREE

generally, but also want a masthead or headline to extend completely across the page as well. In a report, you might reserve two or three column formats only for certain pages, or sidebars.

To vary columns throughout a document, you'll have to divide the document into sections, and then apply different column formats to each section. To create a new section, position your text cursor at the appropriate spot, and choose Section Break from the Insert menu to place a Section marker line. Place your cursor within a particular section, and then choose column settings using either the Ribbon or Section feature. If you'd like to vary columns on the same page, put your cursor in the section following the first column format, choose Section from Format, click the Start button and select No Break.

PAGE NUMBERS

You can tell *Word* to automatically number pages in three ways. Most popular is to choose Print Preview from the File menu, where *Word* responds with a scaled-down version of your pages. Choose the Page Number icon from the window's left side, move the mouse to wherever on the page the numbers should print, and then click. *Word* places page numbers in that location for every page in your document. To place numbers more precisely, you can also choose Section from the Format menu. In the Page Numbers box, click the Margin Page Numbers option to turn the numbering on, and then type in the exact measurements for where numbers should go on the page. The third page numbering method is through *Word's* headers and footers, which I describe on page 78.

Click this icon in Word's Print Preview box to position page numbers throughout your document.

Note: If you ever want to remove the page numbers from your document, you can either drag them off the page in *Word's* Print Preview, or choose Section, and set the page number margin values to 0.

To format page numbers in a custom font or size, choose Style from the Format menu, select the "page number" style, and then specify the format settings you'd like.

Page number formats. *Word* can number pages in five formats—1 2 3, I II III, i ii iii, A B C, and a b c. The default format is the arabic 1 2 3, but you can change it by choosing Section from the Format menu. In the Page

CHAPTER THREE ▾ Setting Up a Document

Numbers box, click the Format button to make your selection.

Page numbers in sections. Remember, if you've created different sections in your document, you can give each section its own page numbering scheme. Place your text cursor within a particular section, and then use the Section feature to make your settings. By the way, each new section in your document can either continue the page number chronology, or start counting fresh from page 1. To start a new count, check the Restart at 1 option in the Section box.

HEADERS AND FOOTERS

To place headers and footers that repeat on every page of your document, choose either Header or Footer from *Word's* View menu. These two features work exactly the same, by the way, except that headers naturally print in the top margin of your page, while footers go in the bottom margin. I'll explain the header function here, and you can apply it to either.

When *Word* calls up its Header window, you can type in any text you'd like. Most headers are only one line long, listing just a chapter number or section heading. But you can type in headers of as many lines as you like. You can also format the header as you would with any other text, choosing the desired font, point size, style, text alignment (left, center, right) and other attributes—call up

Click these icons to stamp your header or footer with current page, data, or time information.

Click Same As Previous if a header/footer should stay the same as in the section before.

Word's Ruler and Ribbon, or Character and Paragraph dialog boxes to help with the formatting.

By the way, *Word* initially formats all headers with a style sheet style called "headers" (or "footers"), which you can permanently modify by using the Format menu's Style command—see page 61 for details on styles.

Notice, also, that you can stamp a header to print page numbers, or the date and time when the document is printed. Just click the appropriate icon at the top of the Header window—for instance, you might type a header such as "Designing a Document, page " and then click the page number icon to insert the appropriate number.

Positioning headers/footers. To specify where on the page your headers and footers should print, choose Section from the Format menu. In the Header/Footer area of the Section dialog box, enter the header's starting point measurement into the From Top box, and the footer's ending point measurement into From Bottom.

Different First Page. Checking this option in the Section box lets you create separate headers and footers for the first page of your document—you'll notice that the First Header and First Footer commands appear under the View menu when you select the option. Since many document formats don't call for headers and footers on first pages, you may want to leave them blank.

Creating Multiple Headers/Footers

Word lets you create different headers and footers for every section in your document (remember, we discussed sections on page 72). Perhaps you've already created various sections—if not, position your text cursor where a new section should begin, choose Section Break from the Insert menu, and *Word* inserts a section marker line. Place your cursor within a particular section, and then choose Header or Footer from the View menu.

> *Word displays its header and footer windows only if you're working in its normal view. In Page Layout view, you'll enter the header/footer directly on the page.*

CHAPTER 4

Writing and Editing Tools

What's Inside

- ▼ The Spelling Checker
- ▼ The Grammar Checker
- ▼ The Thesaurus
- ▼ Hyphenation
- ▼ Word Count
- ▼ Find and Replace
- ▼ Glossaries for Quick Text and Graphics

CHAPTER FOUR ▼ Writing and Editing Tools

Word offers a variety of handy tools to help you write, edit, and otherwise put together documents smoothly and efficiently. Some of *Word's* best and most commonly used features are explained right here.

THE SPELLING CHECKER

Spell checking is hardly new to *Word*, but version 5.0 now sports a new and improved interface that makes checking easier. First, decide what part of your document to check—either place your text cursor at the point where *Word* should begin, or highlight a specific text passage to check. Then choose Spelling under the Tools menu (or type the keyboard shortcut, Command-L) to call up the Spelling window. *Word* starts checking for misspellings in your document immediately.

Finding and Correcting Misspellings

When the checker finds a word that it doesn't recognize, it stops and alerts you with Not in Dictionary, followed by the word in question. In its Suggestions scroll box, the spelling checker also produces a list of legitimate words that closely match your misspelling. And in Change To, it lists the one word most likely to be what you really want. If the Change To suggestion is correct, click Change (hitting Return does the same thing) to insert the correct spelling in your document. Use Change All to similarly change all future occurrences of this misspelling. Otherwise, click a word in the Suggestions box, or type in the correct spelling yourself. Then use Change or Change All.

Word's Spelling window automatically suggests alternatives to misspellings in your entire document, or just a selection of text.

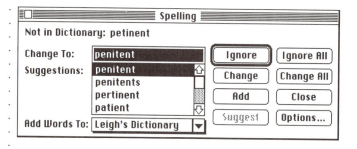

Unrecognized spellings. If the checker stops at a word that is spelled correctly—such as personal names or technical terms—then choose Ignore to pass over that instance. Use Ignore All to pass over every other future occurrence of that word. Or click Add to add the word to the dictionary—more on this in a moment.

Custom Dictionaries

You can create multiple custom dictionaries to hold new terms that *Word's* main dictionary doesn't recognize—for instance, one for medical terms, one for business terms, one for you, and another for your officemate. Any combination of these dictionaries can be accessible at the same time.

Creating dictionaries. To create such a dictionary, choose the Options button from the Spelling window—*Word* responds with the speller's Preferences box, which lets you establish various settings and guidelines for the speller to follow. I'll talk about these options a little later, but for now, focus your attention on Custom Dictionaries. To create your own dictionary, click New and *Word* opens a save file dialog box. Type in a descriptive name—say, *Helmut's Dictionary*—and save. This dictionary is now created, and ready to accept new words. Notice how it's now listed under Custom Dictionaries.

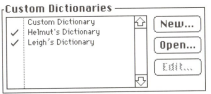

Opening existing dictionaries. There may already be some custom dictionaries on your disk drive. Choose Open to load in existing dictionaries that are not already listed under Custom Dictionaries.

Selecting dictionaries. As mentioned earlier, you can create any number of custom dictionaries, but you might not want to have *Word* refer to them all the time—in fact, too many custom dictionaries slow spell checking down. Fortunately, you can choose which dictionaries for *Word* to refer to and which to ignore by toggling the checkmarks next to the dictionary names.

If you accidentally change a perfectly good word, simply leave the spelling checker, type the necessary correction into your document, and then choose Spelling again. Word picks up where it left off.

Choose Options from the Spelling window to work with custom dictionaries. A checkmark indicates that Word refers to a dictionary as it checks for spelling. Too many checked dictionaries can slow Word down.

> You can use keyboard commands with the speller. Try Return to Ignore, Command-C to Change, Command-S to Suggest, Command-A to Add, Command-O for Options, and Command-Period(.) to Close.

Editing dictionaries. Select the dictionary to edit, and choose the Edit button. *Word* produces a list of the dictionary's contents—you can select and remove words at will.

Adding Words to Dictionaries

To actually add words to a dictionary, make sure you're in the main spelling window. When the checker stops at an unrecognized word, pick a dictionary from Add Words To—you can choose any dictionary that's been turned on through the Preferences box we just talked about. Then click Add, and the checker recognizes the word forever more.

Spelling Options

Click the Options button, and *Word* produces its spelling checker Preferences box, where you can create custom dictionaries and set some simple rules and guidelines for *Word's* speller to follow. We've already talked about custom dictionaries above, so here we'll discuss the remaining options.

Always Suggest. When this is checked, the checker automatically suggests alternative spellings for the unrecognized words it finds. This is convenient, but sometimes slows the spell checking process down as *Word* searches for suggestions. If this is unchecked, *Word* simply stops at unfamiliar words, and it's up to you to click the Suggest button when spelling recommendations are needed.

Spelling preferences which you can set by choosing Options from the Spelling window.

Ignore Words in UPPERCASE/ Words with Numbers. Both of these are self-explanatory. You might want the speller to ignore uppercase words that are, say, abbreviations of states (CA, MA, NY, etc.). Likewise, words with numbers may constitute product model numbers or purchase orders, which you might want the checker to also ignore.

THE GRAMMAR CHECKER

Word 5.0 now scrutinizes the grammar in your documents, looking for subject and verb agreement, pronoun errors, bad punctuation, double negatives, wordiness, and much more. This doesn't mean *Word* will crank out clean, polished prose for you. In fact, you'll probably find many of its grammar suggestions unnecessary, or just plain weird. Nonetheless, the grammar checker *is* handy for catching some of the careless, sloppy writing that we all produce.

Word starts its grammar checking from the point of your text cursor, so position the cursor at the appropriate place in your document. Or highlight a passage of text, and *Word* limits its check to that selection. Take either approach, and then choose Grammar from the Tools menu to call up the Grammar window.

Finding and Fixing Bad Grammar

Word starts checking your prose immediately. When it finds dubious copy, it stops and displays the problem sentence in the Sentence box, highlighting in bold the particular part it's questioning. In Suggestions, you'll find *Word's* recommended action—shorten the sentence, lose a prepositional phrase, etc. Sometimes the suggestion will be simple and straightforward—for instance, to capitalize a word that immediately follows a period. To see how *Word* would correct your prose, click and hold its suggestion in the Suggestions box—*Word* shows its recommended change in the Sentence box. If it looks good, pick the suggestion you prefer (when there's more than one) and click the Change button.

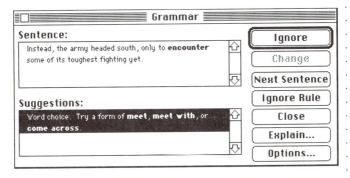

The bold text in the Sentence box is grammatically questionable. Look for advice in the Sentence box.

> 💡 *You can use keyboard commands with the grammar checker. Try Return to Ignore, Command-C to Change, Command-N for Next Sentence, Command-E to Explain, Command-O for Options, and Command-Period(.) to Close.*

Manual changes. Sometimes, a grammar correction is too complicated for *Word* to make on its own (the Change button will be gray, and unclickable). You'll have to leave the grammar window and return to your document—click the document's window in the background, or the grammar window's Close button. Make the necessary changes to your document, and then choose Grammar under Tools once again. *Word* resumes the checking where you left off.

Ignoring advice. Just click Ignore when you don't like *Word's* grammar suggestion, and it will move on. Likewise, Ignore Rule tells *Word* to pass over all violations of a particular grammar rule throughout the rest of its grammar check. Use Next Sentence to pass over an entire sentence, ignoring any other problems in that sentence.

Explain button. Click Explain when you want to know more about the grammar rule or guideline that *Word* is citing. You'll often get a thorough explanation, listing specific rules and helpful examples.

Choosing Explain from Word's Grammar window provides a helpful explanation of the grammar rule in question.

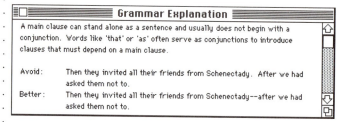

Customizing Grammar Checking

You can tell the grammar checker to behave according to your custom preferences—for instance, to catch split infinitives, or to allow sentences starting with "And" or "But." To customize in such a way, click the Options button in the grammar window. *Word* responds with its Preferences box.

Rule groups. Here are all the possible rules that *Word* applies to your writing. Notice, also, that these are divided into Style and Grammar categories, each with an extensive list (click the respective radio buttons for each list). But while the grammar checker *can* apply all of these rules to your writing, it only recognizes those

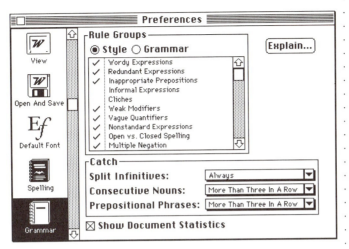

Choose Options from the Grammar window to set your grammar preferences. Among other things, you can define which grammar rules Word applies and which it ignores.

indicated by a checkmark, which you can turn on and off with a simple mouse click. Suppose, then, that you happen to *like* cliches and informal expressions. Just click off these two items' checkmarks and *Word* will pass them over in your prose.

By the way, for an explanation of any of these rules—just what are weak quantifiers, anyway?—click the particular rule, and then choose Explain.

Catch. Here you can define how to deal with split infinitives, consecutive nouns, and prepositional phrases—all potential grammatical troublemakers. Click and hold the appropriate button, and then specify when *Word* should question these occurrences. For instance, you might tell *Word* to stop when it finds more than two consecutive nouns in a sentence, but to ignore any split infinitives.

Show Document Statistics. Check here if you want *Word* to provide various statistics about your writing. For more about this feature, see directly below.

If you're annoyed that the grammar checker also checks for word spellings (you may have already used the spelling checker) then you can turn this feature off by choosing Options from the Grammar window, and uncheck the Open vs. Closed Spelling option in the Style rule group.

Document Statistics

When *Word* finishes checking your document for poor prose, it displays its Document Statistics box, reporting a variety of figures that you may or may not find useful. Most of the statistics are straightforward; word, paragraph, and sentence counts reflect your document's size. Sentences per Paragraph, Words per Sentence and

Chapter Four ▾ Writing and Editing Tools

Characters per Word may help you judge the quality of your prose. For instance, a general rule of good writing is to keep words and sentences short, and these averages help gauge how you're doing.

Document Statistics	
Counts:	
Words	1945
Characters	11680
Paragraphs	15
Sentences	97
Averages:	
Sentences per Paragraph	6
Words per Sentence	20
Characters per Word	4
Readability:	
Passive Sentences	16%
Flesch Reading Ease	50.7
Flesch Grade Level	12.7
Flesch-Kincaid	11.0
Gunning Fog Index	12.9

Most interesting are the Readability statistics, which supposedly indicate how easily people will digest what you write. Passive sentences are usually discouraged, so *Word* reports the total you've allowed. *Word* also tallies four readability scores. According to Microsoft, here's how to interpret the *Flesch Reading Ease* and *Grade Level* statistics:

Flesch-Kincaid is another grade level statistic (a 7 is roughly equivalent to a 70 – 80 above) and there is also the *Gunning Fog Index,* which bases scores on overall sentence length and polysyllabic words per sentence. The higher the score, the harder your writing is to read. Honestly, though, don't feel you have to take these systems too seriously. Good writing is judged by the people who read it, not by a computer algorithm.

Word rates your writing based on a variety of criteria. It's up to you to take this seriously or not.

Skipping statistics. If you don't find these statistics useful, you can always turn off the feature by choosing Options from *Word's* grammar window, and then unchecking the Show Document Statistics box.

Flesch Reading Ease	**Flesch Grade Level**	**Reading Ease**
90 – 100	4	Very easy
80 – 90	5	Easy
70 – 80	6	Fairly easy
60 – 70	7 – 8	Standard
50 – 60	Some secondary school	Fairly difficult
30 – 50	Some higher education	Difficult
00 – 30	Higher education	Very difficult

THE THESAURUS

Word 5.0 now has its own robust thesaurus to replace the *WordFinder* desk accessory used in version 4.0. To use the thesaurus, first position the text cursor on a word you'd like to see synonyms for (you can also highlight the word with a simple double-click). Pull down the Tools menu and select Thesaurus. *Word* responds with the appropriate dialog box, and automatically lists synonyms and similar meanings for your selected word.

Meanings, Synonyms, and Antonyms

Word's thesaurus gives Meanings For a given word, and then gives actual Synonyms. What's the difference? The thesaurus recognizes the subtle differences in meaning for any given word. If you're looking up *appropriate*, do you mean *appropriate*, as in *pertinent*, or as in the verb *to adopt* or *seize*? *Word* is aware of such differences, and it uses Meanings For to list all these possible distinctions. And it uses Synonyms to list the appropriate synonyms for each separate meaning. Click each meaning to see its related synonyms. *Word* also lists Antonyms under Meanings For—click this item for words with opposite meanings. Note, though, that the thesaurus doesn't always suggest antonyms—it depends on the word you're looking up. Likewise, *Word* occasionally lists Related Words, too.

Replacing Words and Other Tricks

When you've found the perfect word in either *Word's* suggested meanings or synonyms, click the item and

> Sometimes you have to coax the thesaurus to find all possible meanings and synonyms. If it doesn't make many suggestions for a particular word, then try its singular or plural form, or a different tense.

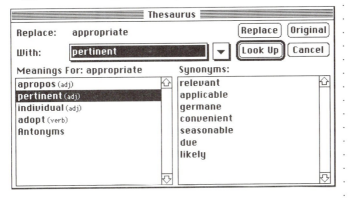

> Highlight a word, and call up Word's Thesaurus window (under Tools) for alternative word suggestions.

choose Replace. *Word* returns to your document and replaces the original lookup word with your new choice.

Some advice: If you're having trouble finding an appropriate synonym or meaning, remember that each suggested word also has its own set of meanings and synonyms to explore. For instance, if you're unhappy with the the synonyms for *amazement*, then simply click to highlight one such synonym, and then choose Look Up. *Word* produces a whole new set of meanings and synonyms for that synonym. Many suggestions you'll have probably already seen, but some will be different and might be appealing.

Other things to know. If you want to look up a word that isn't listed under Meanings For or Synonyms, you can always type the word into the With box and then click Look Up. Your thesaurus also remembers the words you've looked up previously, and makes it easy to return to them for quick reference. Just click and hold the downwards arrow icon next to the With box to see and recall previous words (remember to click Look Up after selecting such a word). Likewise, you can click the Original button to return to the very first word you looked up.

> *You can use keyboard commands with the thesaurus. Try Return to Look-Up, Command-R to Replace, Command-O for Original, Command-C for Cancel, and the Up/Down, Left/Right arrows to highlight Meanings and Synonyms.*

Hyphenation

Word can automatically hyphenate documents to smooth out ragged margins, or to create even word spacing in justified text columns. To do this, position your text cursor at the point where *Word* should start hyphenating, or highlight a specific text passage intended for hyphenation. Then choose Hyphenate from the Tools menu.

Automatic Hyphenation

For *Word* to hyphenate your document in one fell swoop, just click the Hyphenate All button, and *Word* starts hyphenating immediately (click Hyphenate Selection if you've highlighted a section of text). *Word* finishes by saying it's reached the end of your document, and returns to your text window. You should notice hyphenations at the end of various lines.

Problems with Hyphenate All. While the automatic approach is quick and easy, it's not always foolproof. For instance, *Word* may hyphenate two or three lines consecutively—usually undesirable. More importantly, it may hyphenate words the *wrong way*. *Word* uses a special algorithm to determine syllables and where to place hyphens, and this formula occasionally messes up. For instance, *Word* hyphenates *dictio-nary*, rather than using the proper *diction-ary*.

Semi-Automatic Hyphenation

To supervise the hyphenation yourself, click the Start Hyphenation button rather than Hyphenate All. *Word* presents each hyphenable word found, breaking it into its hyphenable parts, and highlighting the hyphen it intends to make for that particular case. If you're satisfied with its choice, click No Change and *Word* applies the recommended hyphenation to your document, and then moves on. If you're not happy with the suggested hyphenation, just click the mouse between the letters your new hyphen should sit between (even these custom hyphens are allowed only between some, but not all, letters). Click Change and *Word* hyphenates according to your custom preference.

You can hyphenate a word yourself, without Word's help—place your text cursor between the two characters where the hyphen should appear, and then press Command-Hyphen(-). Don't just type the keyboard's hyphen key—Word doesn't recognize this as a hyphen, and might not hyphenate your word as you hoped.

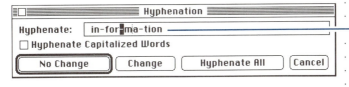

The highlighted hyphen indicates where Word intends to hyphenate. The dotted vertical line indicates the position of the paragraph's margin.

WORD COUNT

One of *Word's* small but wonderful features is its Word Count—especially handy if you write newsletter, newspaper, or magazine articles, where assignments are often based on length in words.

First, decide what part of your document you'd like to count. To do the entire document, just choose Word Count under the Tools menu. Otherwise, highlight a specific text selection and then choose Word Count to call up the appropriate dialog box.

	Word Count		
	Main Text	Footnotes	Total
☒ Characters	20135	2238	22373
☒ Words	3382	397	3779
☐ Lines			
☒ Paragraphs	38	19	57

[Count] [Cancel]

Check these boxes to indicate which text elements to count.

Besides words, you can actually count characters, lines, and paragraphs in your document. You'll see a checkmark next to each variety that *Word* will count—simply click the check boxes on and off to choose the options you'd like. Choose any combination, and then click the Count button (or hit Return). *Word* tallies up the figures and then reports them to you.

FIND AND REPLACE

You're probably familiar with the concept of Find and Replace—you tell *Word* to find an instance of a certain word or phrase, and to put a new word or phrase in its place. Version 5.0 expands considerably on this feature—not only does *Word* find and replace text in this way, but it also looks for special characters such as tabs and page breaks, along with different fonts, sizes, paragraph formats, style sheets, colors, and other text attributes. This flexibility lets you do powerful search and replaces. You might replace two consecutive paragraph marks with one, to remove blank lines in a document. Or search for a specific company name—say, Microsoft—and change all occurrences to bold italics—as in, **Microsoft.**

Using Find or Replace. *Word's* Find and Replace feature is actually two separate commands—under the Edit menu, you'll see Find and also Replace. The distinction is that you'll use Find only to search for an item, but not replace it. On the other hand, use Replace to find an item, and then switch it with something else. I'll concentrate on the more complete Replace command, but you can easily apply the lessons to Find as well.

To use the Replace feature, position the text cursor at whatever point in your document the search should begin, or simply highlight a specific text passage. Then choose Replace under the Edit menu (hitting Command-H does the same thing). *Word* responds with its Replace window.

Finding and Replacing Simple Text

Type the character, word, or phrase that you want to find into the Find What box. Then type its replacement into Replace With. Now you have two options. The first is to click the Replace All button, where *Word* will immediately scour your document and replace all the specified text it finds. The program alerts you when it's reached the end of your document, and then reports the number of changes made in the lower left corner of the document window.

Word reports the number of changes it makes in the lower left corner of the document window.

Semi-automatic replacing. It's convenient when *Word* does all the finding and replacing in one quick pass, but sometimes you'll want to supervise the process—just to make sure that the replacements you specify are appropriate in all cases. Click the Find Next button, rather than Replace All. *Word* will find and stop at the first text case you specified—notice that *Word* highlights the text in the background document window. If you decide a replacement fits here, click the Replace button—*Word* makes the change and then continues the search. If a replacement *isn't* necessary, just click Find Next instead, and *Word* moves on without changing a thing.

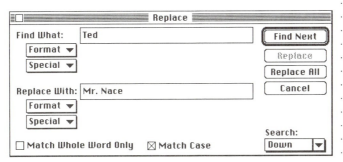

A find and replace for simple text, without any special characters or text formatting.

Other options. Checking the Match Whole Word option tells *Word* to find exact matches of the text you specify, rather than similar matches. Without this checked, the search for "Oak" would find "Oakland" and "Oak tree" as well. Similarly, Match Case finds occurrences with the same lower case and capital letters. And the Search button controls the direction of the search through your document. Choose All to search headers, footers, and footnotes as well.

Special Characters and Other Items

Word also finds and replaces special characters and other unique items, from page breaks to graphics to math formulas. You might also use special characters for wildcard searches of similar words—for instance, you can search for "Gree??" and *Word* finds "Greece" and "Greek." The process works the same way as before, where you first define what *Word* should look for, and then what it should replace with. But instead of typing words into Find What and Replace With, you'll click and hold the Special button to make your selections.

Here's a quick rundown of what each selection does:

- ▼ Tab Mark: finds/replaces tabs, and the space to the next tab stop.
- ▼ End-of-Line Mark: finds/replaces end-of-line marks.
- ▼ Paragraph Mark: finds/replaces end-of-paragraph marks.
- ▼ Page Break: finds/replaces manual page breaks you inserted.
- ▼ Non-breaking Space: finds/replaces special spaces that keep words from being separated by line breaks.
- ▼ Optional Hyphen: finds/replaces hyphens placed by the Hyphenation command, or that you may have inserted. These are real hyphens, *not* dashes.
- ▼ Question Mark: *Word* doesn't ordinarily find/replace question marks. Use this special character to do so.
- ▼ Footnote: finds footnotes in your document.
- ▼ Graphic: finds all graphics and empty frames.
- ▼ White Space: finds/replaces all spaces such as tabs, paragraph and line breaks, section and page breaks.
- ▼ Unspecified Letter: Wildcard letter. "^*nsure" finds "insure" and "ensure."

The special characters and other items that Word can find and replace.

Sometimes a complex find and replace becomes a disaster, changing things you didn't expect. So think carefully about the consequences beforehand. And if you do make a mistake, remember to use Word's Undo command immediately afterwards.

- **Unspecified Digit:** Wildcard digit. "99^#" finds numbers 990 – 999.
- **Caret (^):** Finds ^ characters, which may be used as special commands.
- **Formula Character:** Finds any mathematical formulas created through *Word's* math typesetting feature.
- **Any Character:** Wildcard character. Finds any letter, number, space, or special character.

More about special characters. Notice that *Word* displays a formatting code for each selection that you make—for instance, a *^t* to indicate a tab. This is simply *Word's* own language for working with special characters and items. Also, you can't use all special characters in the replace function. For instance, you can search for a footnote or graphic, because these are generic items. You can't, however, replace information with a footnote or graphic—there's no way to indicate *which* footnote or graphic to replace with.

Text Attributes

Finding and replacing text attributes works just like any other find/replace operation—in Find What, define what *Word* looks for, and in Replace With, define the substitute. But you can now tell *Word* to look for particular fonts, sizes, styles, etc., regardless of the words they make up. To specify these attributes, click and hold the appropriate find or replace Format button, and select either Character, Paragraph, or Styles, according to your preference.

Character. This brings you to *Word's* Character dialog box, where you'll choose the character attributes to find and replace—for instance, New Baskerville, in Italic at 12 points. Notice that *Word* lists your selected attributes in Find What. Now follow the same steps for Replace With—hold Format, choose Character and then the attributes to substitute with—New Baskerville again, but in Bold, and at 14 points. *Word* is now ready to find and replace the attributes you've just specified.

Paragraph. Use the Paragraph option under Format so *Word* can find and replace paragraph attributes, such as line spacing, indentations, tabs, border graphics, etc.

A find and replace for text formatting. This dialog box would find 12 point, New Baskerville characters in the Body Text style, and format them in 9 point, Futura Book, Bold.

Styles. Use Styles to find and replace any styles in *Word's* style sheet—for instance, to find all Subhead styles, and replace them with Headline styles.

Clear. Use this to wipe out all previous attributes you've specified, and start over from scratch.

GLOSSARIES FOR QUICK TEXT AND GRAPHICS

Word's Glossary feature lets you store frequently used text and graphics that you can quickly call up with a few easy steps. For instance, you can create a glossary entry to hold text that you use in your everyday documents, such as a standard copyright notice, an office memo heading, or a closing to a letter. Instead of typing this standard text on each occasion, just apply the appropriate glossary entry and *Word* inserts the text automatically. Likewise, you can use a glossary to store graphics such as a company logo or scanned signature for quick insertion in your work.

Creating a Glossary Entry

In your document window, type the text or create the graphic you'd like to insert in the glossary. Highlight those items, and choose Glossary from the Edit menu (or press Command-K) to call up the Glossary window. In the Name box, type in a name for your new entry—for instance, *copyright notice* or *company logo*—and click the Define button. *Word* lists your new entry in the glossary scroll box, and you're free to return to your document.

By the way, glossary entries can be as short (a word or two) or as long (pages and pages of text) as you like.

Inserting an Entry in Your Document

When you want to insert a glossary entry in your document, first position the text cursor at the point the entry should appear. Then choose Glossary from the Edit menu to call up the Glossary window. Scroll through the window's entry list and select the appropriate entry. Click the Insert button, and *Word* will insert that glossary entry into your document.

Inserting from the keyboard. If you use the Glossary feature often, you'll probably want to insert entries by way of a keyboard shortcut. Again, position the text cursor in your document, and then hit Command-Backspace or Command-Delete (depending on which keyboard model you're using). Notice the bottom-left corner of your document window prompts you with "Name"—type in the name of the desired glossary entry and then hit Return to insert it in your document.

Note: you don't have to type a glossary's full name here—just enough characters so *Word* can distinguish your desired entry from all the others. For instance, to choose the entry *copyright notice*, I'd type in "copy" and hit Return.

> *If you've created glossary entries, and then quit Word, the program will ask if you'd like to save the changes you made to the glossary. Click Yes to save your entries for future use.*

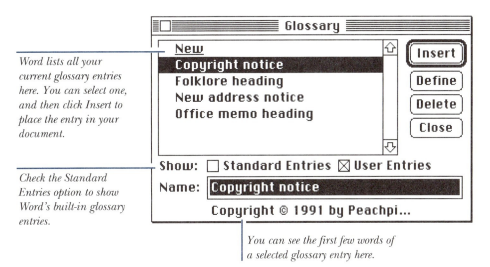

Word lists all your current glossary entries here. You can select one, and then click Insert to place the entry in your document.

Check the Standard Entries option to show Word's built-in glossary entries.

You can see the first few words of a selected glossary entry here.

97

Word's Built-In Glossary Entries

You've probably already noticed that *Word* comes with a number of glossary entries built-in. These are called Standard Entries, and you can see them by calling up the Glossary window (under Edit) and turning on the Standard Entries option.

These entries are mostly helpful for inserting variable information in your document, such as the current time, date, page number, section number, and document summary information. Most of the entry names are self-explanatory, but you can also click on the entry and see its contents listed at the bottom of the Glossary window.

By the way, if you don't want *Word* to list its standard entries in the Glossary window—they *do* clutter things up a bit—then just turn the Standard Entries option off.

> *To edit a glossary entry, first insert it into your document, and make whatever changes you'd like. Then highlight the item again, and choose Glossary from the Edit menu. Select the name of the original glossary entry, and click the Define button.*

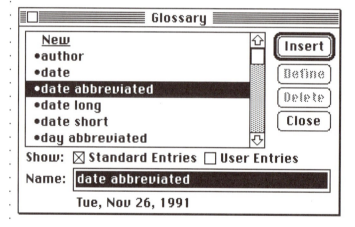

This window lists just a few of Word's built-in glossary entries. To see them, make sure that the Glossary window's Standard Entries option is turned on.

Multiple Glossary Files

Word lets you create multiple glossary files, each with its own unique set of entries. This is especially handy if you find yourself using glossaries on a regular basis, since you can organize the files by task or function. For instance, you might create a glossary file for business addresses, another with math or scientific formulas, and yet another for graphics.

Word always keeps its "Standard Glossary" file open and available to you—this is the file that contains the built-in entries we talked about above, as well as any other entries you make from scratch. Here are the steps for creating and working with new glossary files.

Saving a new glossary file. To save a new glossary file, choose Glossary from the Edit menu. With the Glossary window open, choose Save As from *Word's* File menu. Type in a name for this new glossary file, and click the Save button. *Word* creates the glossary file, including in it all the glossary entries currently listed in the Glossary window.

Opening a glossary file. To open a glossary file, choose Glossary from the Edit menu, and then choose New from *Word's* File menu. This clears all of the entries from the current glossary file (if you don't choose New, *Word* will combine the glossary you're about to open with the existing glossary). Now choose Open from File menu, select the desired file, and click the Open button.

Merging glossary files. To merge the entries of one glossary file to the entries of the current glossary, choose Glossary from the Edit menu, and then choose Open from File. Pick the new glossary file you'd like to add, and *Word* combines its entries with the current glossary.

> *You can add frequently used glossary entries to Word's special Work menu, making them more convenient to select. See page 212 for details about the Work menu.*

CHAPTER 5

Working with Graphics

What's Inside

- ▼ Fundamentals: Graphics Frames and Positioning
- ▼ Word's Built-In Drawing Program
- ▼ Importing Graphics from Other Programs
- ▼ Manipulating Graphics—Cropping, Scaling, and More
- ▼ Simpler Graphics—Borders, Rules, and Shading

CHAPTER FIVE ▾ Working with Graphics

With desktop publishing being so popular, people increasingly complement their documents with graphics, such as technical diagrams, newsletter clip art, or fancy borders or rules. *Word* offers a number of options to satisfy this crowd. First, 5.0 now has a graphics program built-in, so you can create custom graphics on the spot. You can also import ("bring in") art that's been created in other Mac programs, such as *MacDraw II*, or *FreeHand*, and position the images anywhere on your page. In addition, there are no-frills tools for creating graphic borders, rules and background shading to highlight and promote information in your documents.

FUNDAMENTALS: GRAPHICS FRAMES AND POSITIONING

Before tackling anything else, you should understand how *Word* works with graphics in your document—particularly how it positions graphics on your page. In short, *Word* usually puts graphics into graphics frames, and treats these frames as if they were text characters—that is, they can only be positioned in a line of text, along with all other characters. It's hard to visualize, but take a look at the accompanying screen shots and you'll understand that the results are often messy. For instance, since a graphic is actually part of a line of text—just like any other character—*Word* usually upsets your document's line spacing to accommodate it. Likewise,

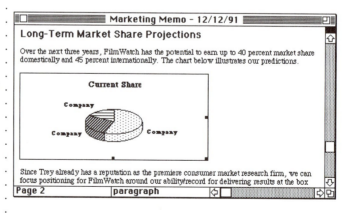

Word's inline graphics, which are positioned on lines of text in your document, are sometimes acceptable, and sometimes not. Here a financial graphic sits on its own text line, and looks fine.

Working with Graphics ▾ CHAPTER FIVE

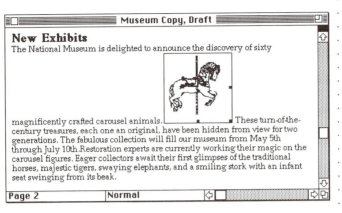

When you'd like to incorporate graphics into text, Word's inline graphics often make a mess. Notice how the graphic here sits on a text line, like any other character.

this approach bars you from placing graphics anywhere on the page, or wrapping text around a graphic, which is crucial in many layouts. These graphics are known as "inline graphics," since they're based in lines of text.

A better way to position graphics. Good news: these limitations only apply when *Word* takes the inline approach to placing graphics. You can also use *Word's* Frame feature to place graphics anywhere on the page, fairly easily, and without compromising your layout. Adopting this tactic is actually a recommended approach, and I show how to position items on page 148. But just remember that when you create graphics from scratch, or import them from other programs, *Word* will, by default, treat them as inline graphics.

And yet another way. To gain more flexibility in positioning graphics , you can also use *Word's* special Table feature. You can easily place graphics and text in bordering cells of a table, and hide the table's outlines so it looks like these items are simply side-by-side, or stacked, or however you'd like to arrange them. See page 64 for more details about setting up tables.

Sometimes you can mix text and graphics by arranging them in table cells, as in this example.

103

CHAPTER FIVE ▾ Working with Graphics

WORD'S BUILT-IN DRAWING PROGRAM

An empty, but selected, graphics frame. Those three handles let you resize the frame and its graphics. See page 111.

Before you can start drawing graphics, you have to first create a frame to hold those graphics. *Word* creates its frames at the location of your text cursor, so position your cursor in the appropriate place. Choose Picture from the Insert menu and *Word* responds with a file selector dialog box. Now click the New Picture button—*Word* places a picture frame at the point of your cursor, and then opens its drawing window.

You can also create a graphics frame with *Word's* Ribbon, if you have it turned on (see page 46 for an explanation). Click the Ribbon's Picture button (it depicts various shapes, and is located on the Ribbon's right side), and Word responds by placing a frame at the point of your text cursor, and then opens its drawing window.

Drawing a Graphic

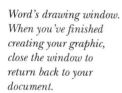

Click this button on Word's Ribbon to create a graphics frame and open the drawing window.

Take a close look at Word's drawing window, and notice particularly the icon palette on the window's left side. These are your drawing tools, which you can activate with a simple click of the mouse. To start drawing, click a shape from the palette—the rectangle, for instance—and move your mouse pointer into the drawing window. When you're ready to put a shape down, just click and

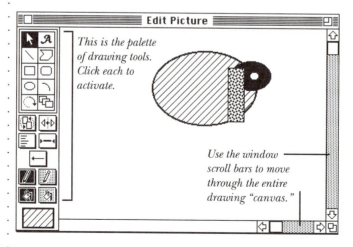

Word's drawing window. When you've finished creating your graphic, close the window to return back to your document.

104

hold the mouse button—drag the mouse around a bit, and W*ord* draws the outline of your shape. When you've reached the right size, release the mouse button and *Word* places your new graphic on-screen.

Manipulating Graphics

Once you've created a graphic in *Word*, you can always change its shape, size, color, and other characteristics. First, select the shape to change—click the Selection tool arrow in the tools palette, and then click anywhere on the border of a graphic (when you select a graphic, it becomes bordered by a number of "selection points"— look for these to confirm your selection).

By the way, you can select multiple shapes, rather than just one, by holding down the Shift key, and then clicking the desired shapes one after the other. You can also click your mouse, and while holding down the button, drag a selection box around multiple shapes.

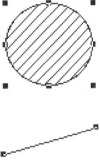

Some selected shapes.

Moving shapes. To move a graphic with the Selection tool arrow, just click and hold the mouse anywhere on the graphic's border. Drag the mouse to move the graphic around, and release at the desired postion (if you've selected multiple shapes, all will move with the mouse). If you hold down the Shift key while moving a graphic, *Word* restricts its movement to purely vertical and horizontal directions—no diagonals. Try it out.

Resizing shapes. To resize a graphic, use the Selection tool to click and hold one of the graphic's selection points. Drag with the mouse, and let go when you have the right size.

Other changes. You can make other changes to graphics by selecting them, and applying *Word's* other drawing tools. See below.

Drawing Palette Tools

Here's a run down of what each of the W*ord's* drawing tools does.

 Selection tool. We spoke about this above. Use this tool to select, resize, and move graphics.

Text tool. Use this tool to place text in the graphics window. With the text icon selected, click anywhere in the graphics window, and *Word* responds with a blinking text cursor. Type your text, and *Word* will wrap the text flow to a new line as it approaches the window's edge. *Word* keeps your text in a frame, by the way, and you can resize that frame, and therefore the text's line lengths, with the Selection tool arrow. You can also use the Text tool to highlight existing text and choose a font and point size from *Word's* Font menu. You can't, however, apply any of *Word's* other formatting features.

Line tool. Use this tool to draw straight lines. Click and drag the mouse to define the shape, and release the mouse button to place it on-screen. If you hold down the Shift key while drawing, *Word* creates only perfectly vertical or horizontal lines—no diagonals.

Polygon tool. Use this tool to make shapes of three sides or more, such as triangles and parallelograms. Click (but don't hold) the mouse to set the starting point of your shape. Move the mouse to your next point, and click again to draw a line connecting the two points. You can continue these steps until you finally click a point on top of the very first point you created—this connects all points, and finishes the shape.

Rectangle, Rounded Rectangle, and Ellipse tools. Use these tools to draw their respective shapes. Click and hold the mouse, and then drag to outline the shape. Release the mouse to draw the graphic on-screen. Note: you can draw perfect squares and circles by holding down Shift while drawing.

> 💧 *If you use a single graphic repeatedly throughout a document—perhaps a company logo for your letterhead—you can store it in Word's Glossary for easier access. See page 96.*

Arc tool. Use this tool to draw curved arc lines. Click and drag the mouse to define the arc's shape, and release the mouse to draw. If you hold down the Shift key while drawing, *Word* draws the arc as if it were around an imaginary circle. Try this out to better see what I mean.

Rotate tool. Use this tool to rotate shapes or text you've created. Select the shape to rotate, and click the Rotate icon. Now click and hold any corner selection point of the desired shape. Drag your mouse, and *Word* rotates the outline of your shape on-screen. Release the mouse button when you're happy with the rotation angle. By the way, once you rotate an object, you can't change its size or shape, or edit rotated text. To make such adjustments, use the Flip tool's Undo All Flips and Rotations feature first.

Duplication tool. This tool works like a quick copy and paste feature. Select an object or group of objects, and click the Duplication icon—*Word* puts a duplicate down and to the right of the original. Click the icon again for as many copies as you'd like.

Front/Back tool. This tool comes in handy when two or more shapes overlap—for instance, if a rectangle sits on top, and obscures some text in your graphic. To decide which should item should appear in front and which in back, select one of the overlapping shapes, and then click the Front/Back icon. Your options are simple: choose either Bring to Front or Send to Back to position the shape as you like.

Flip tool. Use this tool to flip graphics horizontally or vertically, as if you were creating mirror images of the graphics. Select a shape, click the Flip icon, and select either the Flip Horizontal or Flip Vertical option. Use Undo All Flips and Rotations if you'd like to bring your shape back to its original orientation.

Text Alignment tool. Use this to Left, Center, or Right align any text you create in the drawing window. Use the Text tool to highlight the specific text you'd like to affect or use the Selection tool arrow to select an entire text box. Click the Text Alignment icon, and then choose your alignment preference. Unfortunately, there's no Justified option.

Line Width tool. Use this tool to set the line widths for shapes. *Word* usually draws lines with a thickness of one point—to change this, simply click the Line Width icon, and choose your desired width. From now on, Word draws everything with this new width. You can also select existing shapes, and then give them a new width in the same manner.

> *You can convert text into graphic images, perhaps to scale and distort for special effect. Highlight the text in your document, press Command-Option-D, and then choose Paste to insert the new text-as-graphic into your document.*

Chapter Five ▾ Working with Graphics

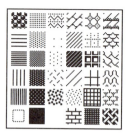

Word's drawing patterns, which you can apply to either lines or fills.

Line and Fill tools. Use these tools to give color and patterns to your graphics. The dark- and light-shaded pen icons let you define, respectively, the color and patterns used to draw the lines of shapes. Likewise, the dark- and light-shaded paint can icons define the color and patterns that fill the inside of shapes. To apply either, select a shape, and then click the appropriate line or fill icons, and choose the desired color or pattern.

Arrowhead tool. Use this tool to place arrowhead pointers at the end of lines. Select a line, and click the Arrowhead icon to place an arrowhead at the beginning, end, both sides, or no sides of a line.

Other Drawing Features

Besides the palette tools, *Word's* drawing program offers a few other features. Don't forget, for instance, the familiar Cut, Copy, and Paste options (under the Edit menu). These work exactly as they do in other areas of the program—just select a graphic with the mouse, and make the desired Cut, Copy, Paste menu selection or keyboard command. Choosing the Clear command under Edit, or hitting the Delete or Backspace key, deletes a selected object. Select All, need I say, selects all the shapes and objects in the drawing window you're currently in. And there's Undo to take back the last action you performed—deleting an object, resizing, coloring, etc.

What Word DOESN'T Do

💡 *Some of your graphics might look better with border frames. See page 111 for details about how to apply borders to your graphics.*

Although *Word* provides the drawing fundamentals, there's a lot that it actually leaves out. A few examples: there is no group feature to let you associate a series of shapes together. There are no graphic alignment tools to line objects up to one another, or position them precisely. There are no rulers or guides, either, nor is there a freehand drawing tool for making unique, non geometric shapes. I could go on. The point isn't to dwell on *Word's* deficiencies—only to say that you might want to use other Mac drawing programs for some projects, and then import their graphics into *Word*. This, in fact, is our next topic.

Importing Graphics from Other Programs

You can import MacPaint, PICT, PICT2, TIFF, and Encapsulated PostScript graphics in two different ways: either load in a presaved graphics file from disk, or copy and paste a graphic from the Mac's Clipboard.

To import a file from disk, choose Picture from the Insert menu. *Word* responds with a file selector box—browse through the various disks and folders until you find the right file. If *Word* doesn't list your file—and you know you're looking in the right place—make sure that the file selector is set to list All Files, All Readable Files, or Graphics Files. Assuming you *do* find your file, select it and click the Insert button. *Word* creates a graphics frame at the point of your text cursor (so put the cursor in the desired location first) and then it plugs the imported graphic into the frame. If the image is too big or small for the frame, just resize it using the frame's three sizing points (for more about resizing on page 111). To edit the image in any way, just select its graphics frame and choose Edit Picture under Edit (or double-click the frame) to bring up *Word's* drawing window.

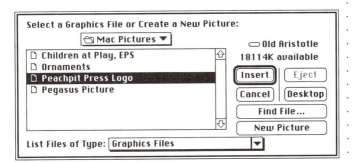

Choosing Picture from the Insert menu lets you choose graphics files from other programs to import.

Using the Clipboard/Scrapbook

You might want to bring some graphics into *Word* simply by cutting and pasting with the Mac's Clipboard (see page 188 for a quick explanation of how the Clipboard works). For instance, you can cut images from a graphics program and then switch to *Word* to paste them into your document. Likewise, you can use the Mac's Scrapbook

CHAPTER FIVE ▾ Working with Graphics

You can use the Mac's Scrapbook—choose it from the Apple menu—to store cut and copied graphics from other programs. If you don't know how to use the Scrapbook, see page 188 for details.

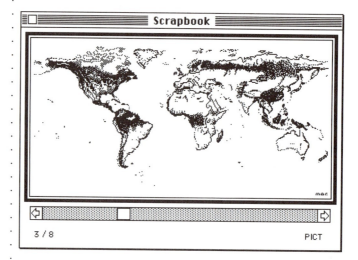

desk accessory—or other similar utilities—to store a library of graphics for pasting at any time.

Be sure the graphic you're importing is already cut or copied into the Clipboard. Position the text cursor at the point you'd like the graphic to appear, and then choose Paste from *Word's* Edit menu. *Word* automatically creates a graphics frame, and copies the graphic into your document. You can resize the image by using the frame's three sizing points (see *Cropping and Scaling Frames* below), or edit it with *Word's* drawing tools by selecting the frame and choosing Edit Picture under Edit (or simply double-clicking the frame).

❗ *If you're not sure what's currently in the Clipboard, choose Show Clipboard from Word's Window menu.*

Importing with Publish and Subscribe

You can create "links" with the graphics you import into *Word*, so if the graphics are ever updated in another program, *Word* automatically reflects the changes in your document. For instance, suppose you import a financial bar chart from your *Excel* spreadsheet. If you ever change the chart in *Excel*—perhaps you receive new financial figures—then *Word* can "sense" those changes, and paste the updated chart into your document.

If you're using Apple's System 7 software, this feature is known as Publish and Subscribe, and it links *Word* to many other Mac programs that also support System 7. Even if you don't use System 7, you may be able to use

Word's QuickSwitch feature with a handful of applications. See pages 191 and 199, respectively, for details.

MANIPULATING GRAPHICS— CROPPING, SCALING, AND MORE

A few notes about how you can work with graphics frames in your document, whether you've created graphics from scratch or imported them from another source. First, you can apply all of *Word's* Cut, Copy, Paste, and Clear commands to a frame, just as you can to text. Select the frame, and then perform whatever operation you like. You might, for instance, cut a frame from one location in your document and paste it to another.

Cropping and scaling frames. You can crop (trim) a graphics frame to hide or reveal parts of its image. When the frame is selected, you'll notice its three sizing handles—simply drag a handle to crop from the image's sides or corner. Don't worry about losing part of an image—you can always enlarge the frame again with the same method. Cropping graphics frames doesn't actually resize the images inside, but scaling *does*. To scale graphics, just hold the Shift key while you're dragging a frame's sizing handle. Drag the corner handle, by the way, if you want to scale in proportion to the graphic frame's original dimensions.

SIMPLER GRAPHICS—BORDERS, RULES, AND SHADING

Its drawing tools aside, *Word* lets you add other modest graphical embellishments to your documents, such as borders (aka frames), line rules and background shading to call attention to important passages, highlight table information, or frame graphics.

To apply these graphics, select the desired text, table area, or graphic, or position your cursor in the paragraph you'd like to affect (by the way, *Word* only applies

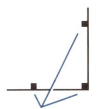

Click and drag one of these sizing handles to size the graphics frame, but not the image that it holds. To resize the image itself, hold Shift while dragging one of the handles.

💡 *When scaling (resizing) graphics, some MacPaint and TIFF images may become rough and distorted. This is a function of the MacPaint and TIFF file formats, not Word. To avoid distortions, try to save the images in a different format, such as PICT or EPS.*

Chapter Five ▼ Working with Graphics

This area represents the text or table you've selected. You can apply a border by clicking the desired side, and then choosing a line style.

Click the Box and Shadow icons to create an instant border with the current line style. Use None to erase a border.

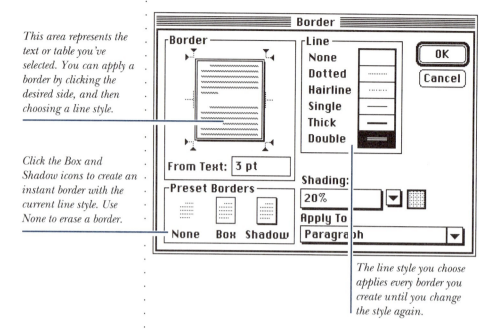

The line style you choose applies every border you create until you change the style again.

border graphics to whole, rather than portions of, paragraphs). Then choose Border from the Format menu, and *Word* responds with its Border dialog box.

Border Basics

Notice the Border box area, and how it represents the text passage, table area, or graphic you selected. In the Preset Borders area, click either the Box or Shadow icons, and the Border box becomes framed on all four sides. You've just created a border for your text.

Line styles. *Word* initially creates single-line borders about one point thick. To apply a different line style, just click the appropriate icon in the Line area—dotted line, thick line, and double line are some of your options. You'll also have to create the border again in that new line style—click None in the Preset Borders area, make sure you've selected the desired line style, and then click the Box or Shadow icon.

❗ *To Remove Borders, just select the bordered text, table, or picture, choose Border from the Format menu, and click the None icon in the Preset Borders area.*

Customizing borders. Borders don't have to frame a passage on all four sides. In the Border box area, click one of the border sides surrounding the representative text passage. *Word* highlights this side alone (two little arrows indicate the side you've selected). Now you can give this particular side its own line style—you might choose *none*, so the border doesn't appear on that side, or *double* or *dotted* to lend a different look. You can do this for each of the border's sides—by being so selective, in fact, you can create rules (simple horizontal or vertical lines) rather than multisided frames. You can also set a different From Text value for each border side (see right below).

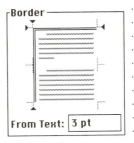

Here I've applied a border to only two selected sides.

From Text. Sometimes a border can crowd nearby text. To put more space between border and text, type a value, in points, into the From Text box (usually two or three points will do).

Apply To. Click this button to specify which elements your border graphics should apply to. Sometimes the button is shaded and non-selectable, so you'll have no choice in the matter. On other occasions, particularly if you're working with tables, you'll be able to apply borders to selected cells, rows, columns, the entire table, and so on. See the section below for details on applying borders to these various elements.

Applying Borders to Paragraphs and Tables

Applying borders can become fairly complex depending on the type of text selection you've made. If you've selected a single paragraph, or a single cell in a table, then creating a border is simply a matter of deciding the sides to border that single item on.

What's complicated is that *Word* lets you select multiple paragraphs, and larger areas of tables, such as a range of cells, or entire columns or rows. When you've selected multiple elements like this, it's not as easy to tell *Word* how to border them. For instance, if you've highlighted multiple paragraphs, you have to decide whether to border the entire selection as a whole unit, or to also place border lines between each paragraph in the selection. It gets worse with tables: if you've highlighted an entire table in your document, you can choose to

You can build border formatting into a style sheet style, so you don't have to specify various settings every time you'd like to apply a border. Just apply the border style instead (see page 61 for details about styles).

Chapter Five ▼ Working with Graphics

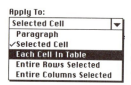

Click the Apply To button to choose which elements your borders will affect.

border the four outer sides of the table, or border the individual rows and columns that make up that table, or separately border each cell in the table (if it sounds a little confusing, that's only because it *is* confusing).

Depending on the elements you've selected, you'll use the Apply To button to specify which elements you'd like to affect in the selection—for instance, if you had selected a single cell in a table, you could use the Apply To button to affect only that cell, its entire row, its entire column, or the whole table it's a part of. What's more, depending on the selection you make, *Word* uses a unique Border box area to represent your selection, and allows you to specify how exactly to border it. Here are some of the Border box areas you're likely to encounter when bordering multiple paragraphs, and tables.

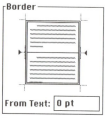

You'll see this box when you've selected multiple paragraphs. The selected line indicates a border between paragraphs.

You'll see this box when you're applying borders to a single cell in a table.

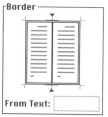

You'll see this box when you're applying borders to rows in a table. You can place a border line between columns of the rows.

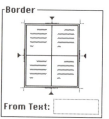

You'll see this box when you're applying borders to multiple rows and columns. You can place border lines between either columns or rows.

Shading Text and Tables

Through *Word's* Border feature, you can apply a gray shade to the background of text and tables you've selected (you don't have to have created a border to do this, although you can mix a gray shade with a border). First select the paragraphs or table cells, columns, rows, etc. that you'd like to shade. Choose Border from the Format menu, click and hold the dialog box's Shading button, and pick your desired shade. Some advice: shades higher than about 30% often make overlaying text hard to read.

Some shades in Word's repertoire.

CHAPTER 6

Book and Reference Tools

What's Inside

- ▼ Making a Table of Contents
- ▼ Making an Index
- ▼ Automatic Footnotes
- ▼ Outlining with Word
- ▼ Linking Documents in a Series

Chapter Six ▾ Book and Reference Tools

If you're producing a book, or some other long, involved document in *Word*, or if you need to annotate references within your writing, then this chapter is for you. *Word's* table of contents and indexing feature can help you ease the task of putting together reference information typical in books and long documents. Likewise, its Outline feature is handy for organizing facts, figures, and ideas into a logical, sensible format, and *Word's* Footnote capability handles all the numbering, renumbering, and formatting of reference notes throughout your document. You might also be interested in *Word's* Document Series feature, which lets you link multiple *Word* files—separate chapters, for instance—into a single document.

MAKING A TABLE OF CONTENTS

Word takes two approaches to building a table of contents for your document. The first involves two basic steps: throughout your document, you'll insert special codes that indicate the headings or passages that you'd like to appear in the table. It's simply a matter of marking items so *Word* recognizes them as table of contents

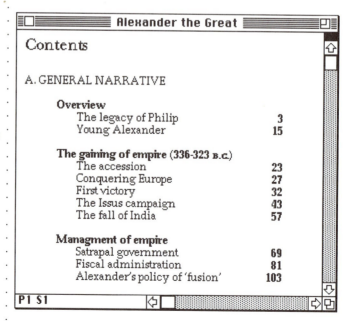

Word can quickly create a table of contents based on the headings in your document.

entries. With all of these special codes in place, you'll issue a compile command—*Word* runs through the document, finds all the entries, notes their page numbers, and then assembles this information into a table of contents. The table is inserted as a new page at the front of your document (in fact, the table is formatted as a new section in your document—see page 72 for an explanation of sections).

That's the first method. The second is handy if you've created your document using *Word's* Outline feature (see page 72 for more details). If you have, then be sure to read the section below, *Making a Table from an Outline.*

Creating a Table of Contents Entry

Much of your table may simply list the various subject headings that appear throughout your document—for instance, chapter and section headings, subheadings, and so on. It's common for many tables to list these headings verbatim, just as they appear in your actual manuscript—for instance, the heading for this section you're reading right now—*Creating a Table of Contents Entry*—would be listed in the table exactly as *Creating a Table of Contents Entry*, followed by a page number.

If your table calls for a verbatim listing like this, then you have it easy.

Inserting TOC codes. Find a heading that you'd like referenced in your table, and highlight it. Now choose TOC Entry from the Insert menu. If you're paying close attention, you'll notice that *Word* responds by inserting a special code—.c.—in front of the text you selected. This is its way of earmarking your text for the table of con-

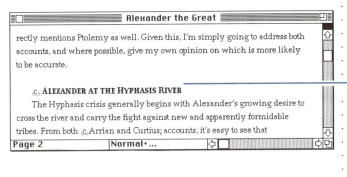

Notice the .c. code inserted in this heading. The code marks the heading for inclusion in your table of contents.

tents. Notice, also, that the code features a dotted underline—this indicates it's formatted in the Hidden text style, which means that it appears on your screen, but won't print in the actual document.

> 💡 *If you don't see the .c. codes you've inserted, Word's Preferences may be set to not show Hidden text. Choose Preferences from Tools, and then click the View icon to make sure.*

By the way, if you had selected an entire paragraph of text, such as a heading on its own line, then *Word* places on the .c. code into that text. But if you selected a text passage that's part of a larger paragraph, then *Word* inserts the .c. code at the beginning of your selection, and also puts a semicolon (;) at the end of the selection. This is just to keep track of where the selection ends in the larger paragraph.

Making Entries Not in Your Text

Sometimes, you'll want to make table of contents entries that aren't based verbatim on the text in your document. For instance, you'll want to reference a passage under a certain heading without the actual heading ever being mentioned in the passage itself. To do this, you'll first insert a TOC entry code, and then tell *Word* how you'd like the text to be listed in the table of contents.

> 💡 *To remove a contents entry, just highlight and delete the appropriate .c. and semicolon codes. If you ever want to remove a batch of entries, you can use Word's find and replace feature to find and replace any text in the Hidden style.*

In your document, just position the text cursor at the spot where you want to make a reference—don't highlight anything, just place the text cursor at the beginning of the reference. Now choose TOC Entry from the Insert menu. *Word* responds by inserting a .c. code, followed by a semicolon, and then places the text cursor between these two codes. Now just type the table of contents heading that the text should be referenced under. For instance, to place a passage under, say, the heading, "Napoleon and Josephine," my TOC entry would read ".c.Napoleon and Josephine;". Remember, you have to type the heading between the .c. code and the semicolon. Remember, too, that this entry is formatted in Hidden text (look for the dotted underline), so it's seen on-screen, but doesn't print on paper.

Multilevel Entries

Word lets you organize the table of contents entries in up to nine levels—for instance, one level for chapter title entries, another for sections, then subsections, etc. When

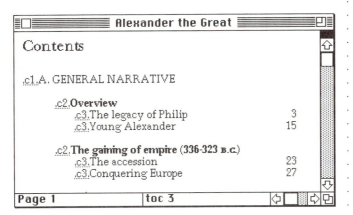

Notice how each heading level has its own unique .c. code—.c1., .c2., .c3. Each code number represents a hierarchical heading in your table. .c1. signifies main headings, .c2. subheadings, and so on.

you compile your table, *Word* indents each entry level accordingly, reflecting the subject organization of your document.

Specifying an entry's level means typing a level number after the "c" in the entry's TOC code (.c1., .c2., .c3., etc.). For instance, if I wanted to assign the heading "Multilevel Entries" to the third entry level, its entry code would be ".c3.Multilevel Entries;".

Compiling the Table of Contents

When you've made all the entries for your document, you're ready to compile the actual table of contents. Choose Table of Contents from the Insert menu to bring up the appropriate dialog box.

Collect. Your first task is to tell *Word* which type of references to collect for your table—either those that you've tagged with the TOC Entry command, or those from your document's outline. We've only talked about the

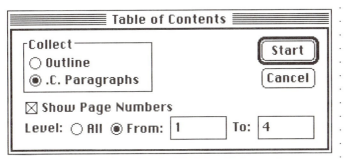

Choosing Table of Contents from the Insert menu lets you generate a table based on the .c. codes you've inserted, or based on your document's outline. I talk about generating a table from an outline on page 122.

first variety, so make sure to select the .C. Paragraphs option in the Collect section of the dialog box. I talk about compiling the table from an outline on page 122.

Show Page Numbers. Check this if you want your table of contents to show the corresponding page numbers for your various entries. I can't think of a reason why you wouldn't.

Level. Here's where you specify which particular TOC entry levels to list in your table (remember, *Word* supports up to nine distinct levels). Chances are, you'll want All listed, but on other occasions, might want to be more selective.

When you've made the appropriate choices, click the Start button in the Table of Contents dialog box. *Word* responds by searching your document for all the TOC entries you've made and notes their page numbers. Then it assembles all this information into an indented table of contents, and places the table in a new section at the top of your document. By the way, make sure you understand *Word's* Section feature, which lets you apply different page layout, page numbering, and other formatting schemes to various parts of the same document. See page 72 for details.

Making a Table from an Outline

If you've organized your document with *Word's* Outline feature (see page 137), you can forgo the routine of entering codes for each table of contents entry you'd like to make. Instead, you'll quickly assemble a table based on the various subject headings in your outline.

Remember how you created different outline levels for the various headings and subheadings in your outline? It turns out that these heading levels correspond to *Word's* nine table of contents entry levels—for instance, *heading 1* in the outline matches the *.c1.* level in the table of contents.

All you have to do is simply compile the table of contents based on these outline headings. To do this, choose Table of Contents from the Insert menu. In the Collect section, choose the Outline option, rather than .C.

> 📍 *If you compile a table of contents, and then edit your document, make sure to recompile the table, since page number references may have changed during your editing.*

> 📍 *If you're bold, you can actually use Word's built-in heading styles to format your ToC without using an outline. Format Word's outline heading styles however you like, and use them to format the headings in your document. Then tell Word to build your ToC from an outline, rather than .c. paragraphs.*

Paragraphs. Then specify whether the table should list all of the outline's heading levels or just a range (you might not want to list some of the more obscure levels). Finally, click the Start button and *Word* assembles your table at the top of your document.

Formatting Your Table of Contents

You'll probably want to fine-tune the look of your table so it's visually pleasing, easy to read, and consistent with the rest of your document's formatting. To do this, you'll use *Word's* Style Sheet feature. If style sheets aren't familiar ground to you, then turn to page 61, and start reading immediately. Style sheets are perhaps *Word's* most valuable asset, no matter what kind of word processing work you do. But for creating a table of contents, they're especially important.

Assuming you *are* comfortable with the style sheet concept, you'll be glad to know that *Word* assigns a separate style to each entry level that's used in your table. Each style is named *toc x*, being numbered sequentially according to the entry level it represents—for instance, if you've created a table with three entry levels, you'll find the styles *toc 1, toc 2, toc 3* in the style sheet.

You can convert text into graphic images, perhaps to scale and distort for special effect. Highlight the text in your document, press Command-Option-D, and then choose Paste to insert the new text-as-graphic into your document.

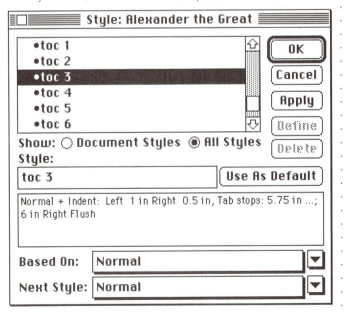

By using Word's Style feature, you can custom format your table of contents headings so they print however you like. For instance, you might set the first level headings of your table to print in New Baskerville, 16 points, Bold, with Small Capitals.

Formatting an entry level simply means defining its corresponding style. Since I explain how to do this on page 61, I'll just summarize here: choose Style from the Format menu. Select a *toc* style, and then set the specific formatting information you'd like—font, point size, indentation, tabs, line spacing, and so on. Maybe you'll set the *toc 1* style to All Caps, Bold. Or format *toc 3*— perhaps for subsections—in a smaller point size, and indent it well into the margin. It's all up to you.

Section formatting. Remember also that *Word* created your table of contents as a new section at the beginning of your document. This means you can format the table's section independently from the rest of the document— perhaps you'd like to change the page numbering to roman numerals, or format the table to print in two or three columns. This is all possible by positioning your cursor in the table's section, and choosing Section from the Format menu. See page 72 for more details.

Creating Multiple Tables

You may want to create more than one kind of reference table in your document—for instance, you might require a table of contents, as well as a table of illustrations. You can create multiple tables in one of two ways.

The first way works if you've used *Word's* Outline feature to organize your document's various subject headings. If you have, then follow the steps for creating a table of contents from your outline (I talked about doing this on page 122). This takes care of your first table. To make a second one—say, of illustrations—use the *.c.* code method to mark all the items designated for the second table. Then you'll compile the second table by following the steps we discussed in the section *Compiling the Table of Contents*, above. While compiling, *Word* will ask if you want to replace the first table you created through your outline. Choose No.

The second way to create multiple tables also involves the *.c.* code method. Remember that you can choose the level of any entry you make by designating the *.c.* codes as *.c1., .c2., .c3.* (on up to *.c9.*). It's unlikely, though, that your table of contents will require all nine entry levels—

three or four will probably do. So reserve the first few levels for table of contents entries, but recruit the remaining entry levels for marking entries for whatever other tables you're creating. For instance, mark any illustrations with the *.c5.* level, and perhaps any charts with *.c6.*

When you've finished marking, you'll use the Table of Contents under the Insert menu to compile a table three times. In the first instance, specify the entry levels that apply to the main table—say, 1 through 4. The second time, specify the levels targeted for the next table, and so on. Remember as you compile additional tables to choose No when *Word* asks to replace the existing one.

MAKING AN INDEX

Creating an index for your document is a lot like creating a table of contents. It's basically a two-step process: first you insert special codes to mark the various words, phrases, and passages that belong in your index. Then you'll issue a compile command so *Word* assembles the marked items, notes their page numbers, and then lists all this information in an index form. The index is inserted as a new page at the end of your document (in fact, the index is formatted as a new section in your document—see page 72 for an explanation of sections).

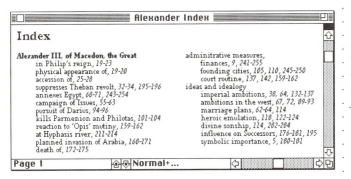

Word creates an index based on special codes you insert throughout your document. The codes mark words and phrases for inclusion in the index later on.

Chapter Six ▾ Book and Reference Tools

Creating an Index Entry

When you've found an item that you'd like to index, the first step is to highlight it, whether it's a single word or multiple words. For instance, I might highlight single-word terms like *California,* or bigger entries like *Empire State Building.* With the entry highlighted, choose Index Entry from the Insert menu.

Notice that *Word* responds by inserting its special index code into the text you selected—the code reads ".i.". If your highlighted text is part of a larger paragraph, then *Word* also inserts a semicolon (;) character at the end of the selection to indicate where the index entry ends. Also notice the dotted underline beneath the index code. This tells you that the code is formatted in Hidden text—you can see it on-screen, but it won't actually print in your document.

At any rate, by inserting these .i. codes, you've tagged your text for the index. When you compile the index, *Word* will list those terms you've marked—say, *California,* and the *Empire State Building.*

Indexing Entries Not in Your Text

Sometimes, you'll want to make an index entry without highlighting and marking specific keywords for the index. You might want to index an entire passage under an entry word that doesn't actually appear in that passage—for instance, index a paragraph about genes and DNA under the entry, *Biotechnology.*

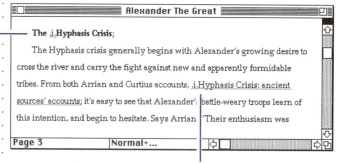

Notice the .i. index code and semicolon in this heading.

I've created another index entry here. This one features two levels, so that the main index entry is "Hyphasis Crisis," with a subentry of "ancient sources' accounts."

To do this, place your text cursor in a passage you'd like to index under your own keyword entry, but don't highlight anything. Choose Index Entry from the Insert menu. *Word* responds by inserting its .i. code, probably followed by a semicolon, and places the text cursor between these two codes. Now type the index entry for the passage—in our example, it would be *Biotechnology*. Just remember to type your entry between the .i. code and the semicolon.

Creating Subentries

So far, we've talked about creating single level index entries, but you can also create up to seven levels of subentries in your index. For instance, you might want to index an entry not simply as *San Francisco*, but as *California: Bay Area: San Francisco*.

To do this, you'll follow the steps used in the section above, *Indexing Entries Not in Your Text*. To summarize: place your text cursor at the point you'd like to make an entry, and choose Index Entry from Insert. Then, in between the .i. code and semicolon, type your multiple entry levels, separating each entry with a colon (:). You'll want to type them in the order of main level entry, second level entry, third, and so on. For example, a second level entry would look like ".i.White House: Oval Office;" while a third level entry would be ".i.California: Bay Area: San Francisco."

Combining Index and Contents Entries

You'll often want the same text entry to appear in both your index *and* table of contents, if you've got one. How to go about it? If your index entry is a single level one—such as ".i.California;" then you can just combine the index and TOC codes into one entry. For instance, to put "California" into the index and contents, you'd first make the contents entry (see page 119) and then add an additional index code so the whole entry reads ".c..i.California;". Notice how the entry combines both the ".c." contents code and the ".i." index code.

If your index entry calls for multiple levels, though—as in "California: Bay Area: San Francisco"—you'll have to make two separate entries. First make a contents entry—say, ".c.California;". Then make the index entry in the same area, following the steps outlined above in *Indexing Entries Not In Your Text*. Just type in the entry and subentries as you normally would. The form should follow something like ".i.California: Bay Area: San Francisco;".

Compiling Your Index

With all your various entries made, you're ready to compile your index. Choose Index from the Insert menu to bring up the appropriate dialog box.

Format. *Word* can create what it calls Nested and Run-in indexes. Nested indexes are most common—*Word* lists each entry on a separate line, with subentries indented under their related topics. Run-in indexes, on the other hand, list all entries and subentries on a continuous line, with the various entries separated only by semicolons. Although I find Run-ins harder to read, they do save space, if that's an issue. But choose whichever form you'd like *Word* to compile.

Assemble your index when you've finished all text editing and are ready to print. If you create an index first, and then go back and change your text even a little, the index's page numbers could become inaccurate.

A Nested index (top) is usually easier to read, but a Run-in format saves space by listing all related index entries in one continuous block.

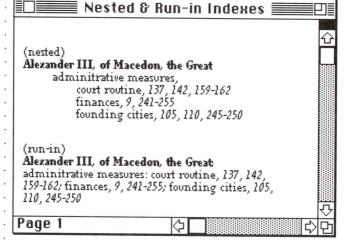

Index Characters. This section lets you specify which particular alphabetical headings *Word* should index. To create a full index, you'd choose the All option (for the letters A through Z). In other instances, you might want to index a certain group of letters, like P through T. If so, just enter the letter range into the From box.

When you've made your selections, click the Start button in the Index dialog box. *Word* searches your document for all index entries and notes their page numbers. Then it assembles this information in an index format, and places the index in a new section at the end of your document.

Index Arguments

Word's index arguments give you greater control over how indexed information is presented. For instance, you can define how page numbers are formatted, list page ranges rather than single pages, and make cross references to other entries. It's simply a matter of adding a few extra characters to the standard .i. index codes.

Formatting page numbers. You can tell *Word* to print an index entry's page number in **Bold**, or *Italics*, or ***both***. For bold, insert a "b" into the entry's ".i." code—the proper form is to place this extra character between the .i and the last period (.). For example, the entry ".ib.California;" would index the entry as "California **32**" (I'm using that random page number just as an example). Notice the page number is in bold. To italicize the page number, just insert an "i" into the ".i." code—".ii.California;" would produce "California *32*" in the index. And ".ibi.California;" makes "California ***32***".

Indicating page ranges. Sometimes you'll want to list a page range for index entries, such as "California 32–40". To do this, make an index entry in the text where your range begins—for instance, at the first mention of "California" in your document. Now add an open parenthesis character to the entry's .i. code. The proper form would be ".i(.California;". Then make another entry at whatever point the page range ends, this time adding a close parenthesis character to the ".i." code—the proper form would be ".i).California;". When you compile your index, *Word* lists the entry as "California 32–40" (the actual page numbers depend on where you made the first and last entries, of course).

Referencing other index entries. You might also want an index entry to refer readers to another entry, rather than a page number. The entry "Russia (*see* Soviet Union)" is a good example. To create such a cross-reference, make your standard index entry, and then add a number sign (#) immediately after the index entry text. Type in your cross-reference, and close the code with a semicolon. The proper form would look like this: ".i.Russia# (*see* Soviet Union);".

Formatting Your Index

You can quickly format the look of your index by using *Word's* Style Sheet feature (see page 61 if you're not already familiar with style sheets). For each index entry level you've created in the index (remember, you can use up to seven levels), *Word* creates a corresponding index style in its style sheet—*index 1, index 2, index 3*, and so on. Actually, this is just the case if you've created a Nested index, which lists each entry level on a separate line of the index. If you've adopted a Run-in index instead, then all entry levels are listed on one line. Accordingly, *Word* only needs one style to format these entries—*index 1*.

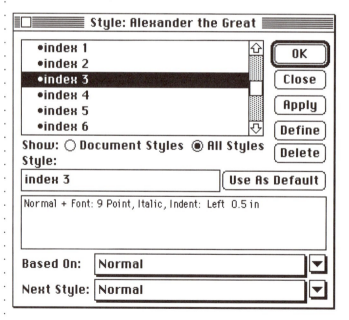

You can use Word's Style feature to custom format index entries. Choose the desired index entry level, and then apply whatever formatting you like—font, size, style, spacing and so on.

Formatting an index level simply means defining its corresponding style in the style sheet. Since I explain how to do this in depth on page 61, I'll just summarize here: first, choose Style from the Format menu. Select an index style, and then set the formatting you'd like—font, point size, indents, tabs, line spacing, and so on. *Word* then applies that format to any corresponding index entry level.

One more note: as you'll see, *Word* initially bases its index styles on the *Normal* style in the style sheet. When you're reformatting each index style, you may want to base each style on the next lowest index style. For instance, base *index 3* on *index 2*, *index 2* on *index 1*, and *index 1* on *Normal*. This way, if you change one index style, the adjustment will be reflected in the following index entry styles.

Section formatting. Remember also that Wo*rd* creates your index as a new section at the end of your document. This means you can format your index separately from the rest of your document. Perhaps you'd like to create new headers or footers, or set the index to print in multiple columns. This is all possible through *Word's* Section feature—read up about it on page 72.

AUTOMATIC FOOTNOTES

Word takes much of the tedium out of managing footnotes in your writing. Basically, you'll insert a footnote entry at whatever point in your document a footnote should appear. *Word* then automatically manages those notes for you—it renumbers them if you later add new notes or delete others, or if you rearrange your document so that the original footnote order changes. *Word* also lets you decide where footnotes appear in the document (at the bottom of a page, on an end page, and so on), and how the notes are formatted.

Making a Footnote Entry

Position your text cursor immediately after the sentence, paragraph, or passage that you'd like to annotate. Choose Footnote under the Insert menu for the footnote dialog box (pressing Command-E does the same thing). In most cases, you'll want *Word* to automatically number the note you're making, since it's already keeping track of how many notes there are in the document. If so, leave the Auto-numbered Reference option checked. However, if you want to assign the footnote your own reference mark, you can type up to 10 characters in the Footnote Reference Mark box. For instance, you might want to use a * or ™ or † symbol as a marker. We'll focus on the automatic reference mark, however.

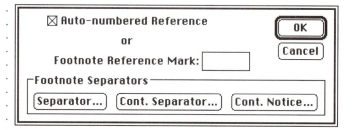

Choosing Footnote from the Insert menu gets you to this dialog box. If you want Word to automatically number your footnotes, be sure that the Auto-numbered Reference option is checked.

Click OK and *Word* inserts the first available footnote number at the point where you positioned your text cursor (the note number will be a superscripted 1,2,3,4). If you're working in Page Layout view, *Word* follows by moving the cursor to the bottom of the page so you can type in your note annotation. But if you're in Normal view, as you'll probably be, then *Word* splits your document window into two window "panes" (see page 39 for more details about this feature). The top pane shows the familiar text of your document, but the bottom pane holds all the footnotes of your document. There you'll notice the new footnote number you've just created, followed by the text cursor. Now type in the actual note annotation. You can apply any font styles such as Bold, Italic, and Underline. You can also hit Return to create a new paragraph in the same annotation.

Book and Reference Tools ▾ Chapter Six

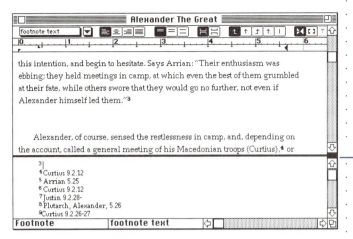

When working in Normal view, Word splits your document into two panes, so you can work with your main text in the top pane, and enter notes in the bottom pane.

Drag this Split bar to adjust the size of the footnote pane, or drag it above the Scroll bar to close the pane.

When you're finished typing the note, just click the mouse in the upper pane of the split window to return to your document and continue writing. Follow these steps for all the notes in your document. Remember that you can insert notes in any order—for instance, insert a new note between two existing ones. *Word* will automatically renumber the notes to reflect this new order.

Removing notes. To remove a footnote, *don't* delete its number and annotation in the footnote window pane. Instead, delete the note's superscripted reference number in your main text (in the document window pane). *Word* then removes the corresponding annotation, and renumbers any notes affected by the change.

The footnote window pane. When you've finished typing in a footnote annotation, notice that the footnote window pane remains on-screen. It's actually linked to the document pane above it, so if you scroll through the document pane, the footnote pane automatically scrolls to display any footnotes that correspond to the text in the document pane. This works in reverse, too, so when you scroll through the footnote pane, the document pane also scrolls to show the text corresponding to the notes in the footnote pane.

Formatting Footnotes

You can custom format your footnote's reference number and annotation text by using *Word's* Style Sheet

You can cut and paste text passages that include footnote references, and Word will automatically renumber its notes to reflect any new order. Just be sure to include a note's reference number in any text you highlight for cutting.

To open the footnote window pane without making a new note entry, just double-click an existing footnote reference number in your main document.

133

You can custom format footnote reference numbers and footnote text by modifying the corresponding styles in Word's Style window.

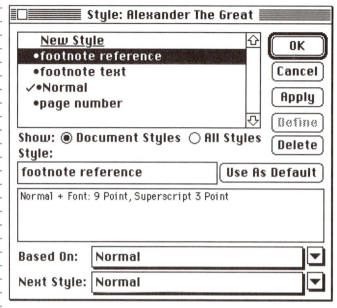

feature (see page 61 for more about style sheets). The formatting for a note's reference number is set by the *footnote reference* style in Word's style sheet, while *footnote text* handles the actual annotation. By choosing Style from the Format menu, you can redefine these styles with your own settings for font, point size, indent, margin, line spacing, and so on. You may, for instance, want to format footnote reference numbers in Bold Italic, while setting the annotation text at a small point size, and with little line spacing.

Where Footnotes Print

Word lets you decide exactly where in your document footnotes should appear—at the bottom of each page, at the end of their section (if you've created multiple sections), or at the end of the entire document. By default, *Word* prints notes at the bottom of the page of their respective references. To change this, choose Document from the Format menu. In the Footnotes area of the Document dialog box, click the Position button to make your choice.

Bottom of Page. Notes print at the bottom of the page that contains its reference mark. This is the default.

Beneath Text. Notes also print on their respective reference pages, but they're positioned directly under the last paragraph of the page, rather than strictly the bottom of the page. For instance, if text ends midpage, then your notes will begin midpage as well.

End of Section. If you've created multiple sections in your document, this option will print your footnotes on the last page of their respective section, rather than printing the notes on their respective pages (by this approach, they really become endnotes, rather than footnotes). Just be sure that the section is set to print endnotes—choose Section from the Format menu, and make sure the Include Endnotes option is checked. If this option isn't checked, the section's respective notes will be held over to the next section that *is* set to include endnotes.

End of Document. Notes print on a separate page at the end of your entire document.

Footnote Numbering Options

If you don't want *Word* to start numbering your footnotes from 1, then you can set the number from where it should start. Choose Document from the Format menu, and type the new starting number into the Number From box.

You can also tell *Word* to number footnotes continuously through a document, or to restart the numbering on every new page, or every new section (if you've created multiple sections in your document). Again, choose Document from the Format menu. In the Footnote area of the Document dialog box, check the Restart Each Page option.

Footnote Separators

When *Word* prints your footnotes at the bottom of a page, it uses a simple horizontal line to separate the notes from the main document text above. The line starts at the left margin of the page and extends about

You can tell Word where to print footnotes, and how to number them, through the Document command under the Format menu.

Chapter Six ▾ Book and Reference Tools

You can modify Word's Footnote Separators by choosing Footnote from the Insert menu, and then clicking the appropriate separator button.

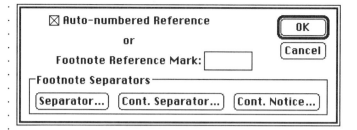

halfway across the page. *Word* calls this line the Footnote Separator. Sometimes the footnotes for one page will be too long, and will run over to the following page. *Word* prints a Continuation Separator line on the page that holds the run-over notes from the previous page. Like the regular Separator, the Continuation Separator divides the notes from the main document, but the line extends fully across the page (whereas the Separator line goes only halfway). How readers will notice these subtle differences is beyond me.

Here's a Footnote Separator line in action. This one happens to be a Continuation Separator, since it appears over footnotes that are continuing from a previous page.

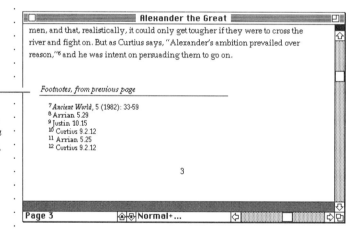

Customizing the separators. In any case, *Word* lets you customize its Separator and Continuation Separator. For instance, you might replace the simple Separator line with text such as "Footnotes...." Likewise, the Continuation Separator line could become "Notes, continued." To customize these lines, choose Footnote from *Word's* Insert menu. In the Footnote dialog box, click either the Separator or Cont. Separator buttons, and *Word* re-

136

You can customize Word's Footnote Separators through these Separator windows. Word uses whatever text and graphics you create as a Separator. In this case, I've added the text "Footnotes, from previous page" to the original Separator line.

sponds with another window containing the separator you've chosen. You can now edit the separator—highlight and delete the line, add text to it, replace the line with asterisks or other symbols, or whatever else. Close the window when you're finished, and *Word* will use your custom separator from then on.

Continuation Notice. You can also set a Continuation Notice for footnotes, which prints below footnotes that will wrap to the next page, and tells readers that the notes continue on the next page. Word doesn't ordinarily print a Continuation Notice, but by clicking the corresponding button in the Footnote dialog box, you can create one to read "footnotes continue on following page" or something similar.

OUTLINING WITH WORD

Word's Outline feature helps you sort out and organize your ideas in a logical, progressive order, just as you did in junior high English. What's more, the outline you create is actually linked to your main document, so you can quickly rearrange the entire document by shuffling information in the outline. Likewise, you can easily format the outline and see that formatting reflected in your document.

To use *Word's* Outline feature, choose Outline from the View menu (or press Command-Option-O). *Word* switches to its Outline view, and adds the Outline command bar to the top of your document's window.

Chapter Six ▾ Book and Reference Tools

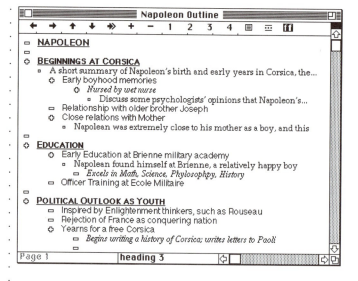

Word's Outline view helps you organize the ideas and points in your document by creating related headings, subheadings, and sub-subheadings.

How the Outline and Your Document Are Related

Before starting with actual outlining, it's important to emphasize how your outline and document are related. The outline isn't a stand-alone organizational tool, but simply another way to view and work with your document (like the Normal and Page Layout views offer different ways to view and work with your document). So when you create headings and subheadings in the outline, you'll see these become headings in your document when you return to the Normal or Page Layout views you're used to working in. The advantage of the Outline view is that by focusing on heading organization, it's handiest for organizing and rearranging ideas. On the flip side, you'll find that while it's good for playing with headings and subheadings, it's not as convenient for entering the main body text of your document. For this, you'll probably want to use the Normal or Page Layout views to add the "meat" to the headings you create in the outline.

🛑 *By creating your document in Outline view, you can easily generate a table of contents based on the outline's headings. See page 122.*

Starting an Outline

The usual approach to outlining is to first organize various headings and subheadings by assigning them to heading levels, so *Word* can rank the headings in the

138

outline. You can have up to 9 heading levels in an outline—*Word* numbers them 1 through 9, with level 1 being the broadest headings, level 2 being subheadings, 3 being sub-subheadings, and so on.

Entering outline headings. Just type in a heading—let's say it's "Napoleon's Birth at Corsica." *Word* assigns the heading to level 1, the broadest, most general level. You can hit Return to end the heading, and move down to the next line, where you can type another heading on the same heading level.

Promoting and demoting headings. When you want to change a heading's level in the outline—to make it a subheading for another heading, for instance—place the text cursor anywhere in that heading. Then click the left and right arrow icons in the Outline command bar (at the top of your document window) to promote and demote the heading, respectively, by one level. Likewise, you can use the up and down arrows on the command bar to move a heading one line up or down in the outline. You'd do this to rank headings, with the most important headings being higher in the outline order.

Click these icons on the Outline command bar to promote, demote, and move headings up and down in the outline.

Once you've promoted and demoted a few headings, you'll notice how *Word* indents each heading level differently, and formats each level with either a unique font, style, or point size. This variety simply helps you distinguish one heading level from the other, and see how the various headings are related to each other.

Heading symbols. *Word* places either a box character or fat cross symbol next to the various headings you create in the outline. These simply tell you whether their respective headings have a related subheading beneath it. The box character indicates there's no related sub-heading, while the fat cross means there is. A smaller box character indicates that the heading is actually body text, which we'll talk about soon.

The fat cross indicates that a heading has subheadings beneath it, while the box character tells you there are no related headings.

Adding Body Text to the Outline

Once you've started to organize your headings, you'll want to add main body text of your document. To enter body text for a given heading, start a new heading line

Click the double-arrow icon on the Outline command bar to demote a heading to body text.

Click this icon on the Outline command bar to toggle between showing just the first line of body text paragraphs, or the whole paragraphs. You might want to see only the first lines of body text to keep clutter of your outline to a minimum.

directly below the heading you'd like to create the body text for. Then click the double-arrow icon on the Outline command bar to convert the new heading line to the body text format. Now type in your text.

You can hit Return to start a new body text paragraph, or you can use the command bar's left and right promotion/demotion arrows to set a new line back to a heading level.

Adding body text in another view. If you have a lot of body text to add, it might be more comfortable to leave *Word's* outliner and return to Normal view—choose Normal under the View menu (or choose Page Layout view, if you like). You'll notice the various headings you created in your outline—position the text cursor at the end of the heading you'd like to add body text to, and hit Return. *Word* begins a new line for your body text, and formats it using the Normal style of its style sheet (you should read up on *Word's* style sheet on page 61). Type whatever prose you have—you can create however many paragraphs, and format the text as you like. When you'd like to return to your outline, just choose Outline from the View menu—*Word* adds the body text to your outline, indenting under the proper heading. Also notice the small box character at the left of each body text paragraph—it's there just to let you know you're looking at text, rather than a heading.

Rearranging Your Outline

It's almost inevitable that as you'll want to rearrange and reorganize your outline as you develop your ideas. This means easily promoting and demoting not only headings, but all their related subheadings as well. For instance, you might have a second level heading with a related third level subheading, and even related level 4 headings. If you promote that second level heading to level 1, *Word* can automatically promote its level 3 and 4 subheadings to levels 2 and 3.

To select a heading and all the related headings beneath it, click the symbol to the left of the heading.

Remember also that by rearranging the outline, you're also rearranging your main document's corresponding headings and body text. You'll see your changes reflected when you return to Normal or Page Layout view.

Promoting and demoting heading families. First, select the heading you'd like to affect by clicking on its heading symbol (the box character or the fat cross to the left of the heading). Notice that clicking a character box symbol only selects that single heading, since a character box indicates there are no related headings. But clicking a cross selects that heading, and all of the subheadings beneath it.

You can cut, paste, and delete headings, and Word will automatically rearrange (by promoting or demoting) the outline's existing headings to reflect that change.

With the appropriate heading or headings selected, click the left and right arrow icons in the Outline command bar (at the top of your document window) to promote and demote the headings, respectively, by one level.

You can also rearrange headings and relations by clicking and holding a heading's symbol to select it, and then dragging left/right or up/down with the mouse. *Word* displays a dotted line moving along with the mouse, indicating the new position you're moving to. Release the mouse button to place the selection in the new spot.

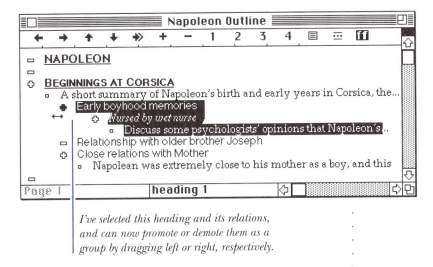

I've selected this heading and its relations, and can now promote or demote them as a group by dragging left or right, respectively.

Collapsing and expanding headings. Sometimes your outline develops so many headings and subheadings that it becomes too long and cluttered, to work with easily. To solve this, you can "collapse" headings so their related subheadings don't appear on-screen. Likewise, you can "expand" headings back to their full-blown state. By the

Chapter Six ▼ Book and Reference Tools

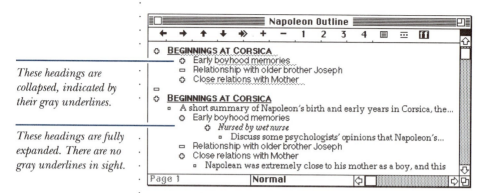

These headings are collapsed, indicated by their gray underlines.

These headings are fully expanded. There are no gray underlines in sight.

+ −

1 2 3 4

Click the Minus and Plus icons on the Outline command bar to collapse and expand selective headings one heading at a time. Click the 1 2 3 4 icons to collapse and expand the corresponding levels of the entire outline.

▤ *Click this icon on the Outline command bar to fully expand the entire outline.*

ff *Click this icon on the Outline command bar to toggle the outline's on-screen text formatting on and off.*

way, when you collapse a heading so its subheadings don't show, *Word* uses a gray underline to indicate that the main heading has collapsed information beneath.

The quickest way to collapse an outline is to click the 1 2 3 4 numbers on the outline command bar—this collapses the outline to the number's corresponding level. Clicking 2, for instance, would collapse the outline so that only level 1 and 2 headings appear (you'll notice the gray underline to indicate collapsed information beneath the remaining headings). Click the expand entire outline icon on the command bar to expand all headings back again.

To collapse all subheadings below a single heading, double-click the heading's fat cross symbol. Double-click again to expand.

To selectively collapse subheadings one level at a time, rather than all together, just place the text cursor in the main heading and click the Minus icon on the command bar. Likewise, use the Plus icon to expand.

Formatting Your Outline

Word formats each heading level in your outline with a distinct style, which is useful for distinguishing one heading group from another. But *Word's* preset heading styles probably won't be suitable for the formatting style of your own document. Fortunately, you can use *Word's* Style Sheet feature to change the formatting for each heading level (see page 61 for more about style sheets). *Word* creates a style sheet style for every heading level

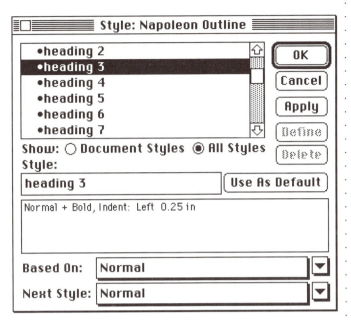

You can format the look of an outline's headings by modifying the corresponding heading styles (heading 1, heading 2, etc.). Choose Style from the Format menu, and make sure that the All Styles option is checked.

that's used in your outline. For instance, if you've got three heading levels, you'll find corresponding styles called *heading 1, heading 2,* and *heading 3.* To set the style for a particular heading level, just adjust its corresponding style. To summarize the steps, first switch to either Normal or Page Layout view. Choose Style from the Format menu, select the appropriate heading style, and then specify the desired font, point size, indent, line spacing, and other values.

Adding heading numbers to your outline. You can use *Word's* paragraph numbering feature to number the headings in your outline—for instance, label first level headings with roman numerals, second levels with alphabet letters, third levels with arabic numbers, and so on. To number your outline, first collapse the outline to show only the heading levels you wish to number (no need to do this if you'd like to number all levels). Highlight the desired part of the outline, and choose Renumber from *Word's* Tools menu. To number the headings in a traditional outline format, type "I.A.1.a.i" into the Format box—this is a little cryptic, but you're nonetheless telling *Word* how to number each heading level. When you click OK, *Word* numbers the outline accordingly. To really understand *Word's* numbering feature, see page 58.

LINKING DOCUMENTS IN A SERIES

If you're building a long document, it may be more efficient to break one huge document file into smaller, multiple files to save memory and keep *Word* running up to speed. You can then link the multiple files into a series—they'll print as a single document with continuous pages.

To create a linked series, open the first document of the series—for instance, the introduction of a book. Choose Document from the Format menu, click the File Series button, and then select the Continue option in the dialog box. This tells *Word* that you're going to number pages continuously across multiple files. Now click the Next File button to call up *Word's* Open dialog box. Choose the next document file you'd like linked to the current one, and then leave the various dialog boxes to return back the *Word's* document window. Save your document, and then open the next document in the chain, and repeat the steps above to link that document to whatever file should follow it. Keep doing this, until you've linked all the proper document files.

The File Series box lets you join the current document in a chain of linked documents. This is helpful for managing large documents, which you can divide into smaller, separate files.

Numbering Items Across the Series

You may notice that the page numbers of the various documents you've linked all start at 1 for each document. Don't panic—when you go to print linked documents, *Word* will automatically revise the page numbers of each to print continuously from the first document in the series.

To print a series of linked documents, see page 185.

Word won't, however, renumber other items in your documents, such as footnotes, lines or paragraphs. You'll have to do this yourself. Start with the first document in your series, and note the last numbered footnote, line or paragraph in the document. Now open the next document in the series and use *Word's* footnote, line and paragraph features to start numbering the items in this document where the previous document left off. For instance, if the first document's footnotes end at 16, then you would use *Word's* Document command to start the next document's footnotes at 17. Likewise, you'd use the Renumber command under the Tools menu to set the starting point for continuing paragraph numbers, and the File Series button (in the Document dialog box) for continuing lines.

Follow these steps for every document in the linked series. Just make sure that you've completed all the editing in the documents beforehand. If you haven't finished editing, and make even one change to footnote, paragraph or line numbering, then you might have to reset all the appropriate starting numbers throughout the linked documents.

CHAPTER 7

Miscellaneous Stuff

What's Inside

- Positioning Text and Graphics
- Making Voice Annotations
- Math Calculations
- Sorting Information
- Print Merge for Form Letters and Mailing Labels
- Merging with Mailing Labels
- Math and Scientific Equations

Chapter Seven ▾ Miscellaneous Stuff

When writing a book, there are always a handful of topics that don't seem to fit any particular chapter, or that belong in number of chapters at once. Hence, a Miscellaneous section. Here I'll talk about a number of unrelated but important topics, from print merging form letters and mailing labels to typesetting equations to recording voice annotations in your documents.

Positioning Text and Graphics

Word lets you position items such as text, graphics, tables, and formulas anywhere on a page, rather than just within the confines of the page's standard text margins. What's more, *Word* also wraps your document's text around these positioned items—like a page layout program does—making this feature invaluable for projects that require even a little layout savvy. For instance, you can place a graphic between two columns of text, or set text headings in the left or right margins of your page. You can also specify a few other settings for positioned items, such as whether to anchor them to the page, or to let them move throughout a document with respect to related text.

Positioning an Item

Positioning an item means putting it in a frame, and then specifying where that frame should go on the page. Luckily, this is accomplished through just one of two commands. You'll use the Insert menu's Frame command to position graphics, tables, equations, and small samples of text such as captions or headers. On the other hand, if you want to position passages of text—anything more than a few words—then you'll probably want to use the Frame command under the Format menu (not the Insert menu). I explain why in the following section, *Positioning Text Passages*.

Positioned items do not appear positioned in Word's Normal view, but they do in the Page Layout view (under the View menu), and Print Preview (under File).

To position anything else, first select the item—click on a graphic, highlight an entire table (or specific rows and columns), or a small selection of text. Choose Frame from the Insert menu, and *Word* switches to its Print Preview mode, giving you a reduced view of the entire

Miscellaneous Stuff ▾ CHAPTER SEVEN

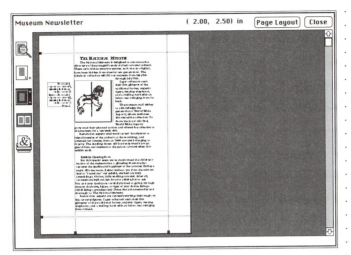

To position graphics and some instances of text, just highlight the desired item, and choose Frame from the Insert menu. Word lets you position the item in this Print Preview mode.

page. Notice how *Word* surrounds the item you've just framed with a dotted frame. Click on or inside the frame, and drag its outline anywhere on the page. When you release the mouse button, *Word* thinks for a few seconds and then moves the frame to the point you specified, wrapping any overlapping document text around it (by the way, you can click anywhere outside the reduced page to make *Word* move the frame immediately).

Space between frames and text. When *Word* wraps text around a frame, it puts white space between the text and frame so the two don't crowd each other. To reduce or enlarge that space, first select the positioned item in your document, and then choose Frame from the Format menu (*not* the Insert menu). Type a new space value in the From Text box.

❗ *To un-position an item, select the item in your document, choose Frame from the Format menu, and click the Unframe button.*

Positioning Text Passages

When *Word* positions items with Insert menu's Frame command, it positions them at their original widths, so they take up as much horizontal space on the page as they would ordinarily. Unfortunately, this usually isn't acceptable for text passages. When you select a text passage or paragraph to position, you're selecting it at its width on *Word's* Ruler—chances are, the passage will be several inches across. But you'll probably want to position that text at a different width—for instance, to fit in a

149

CHAPTER SEVEN ▼ Miscellaneous Stuff

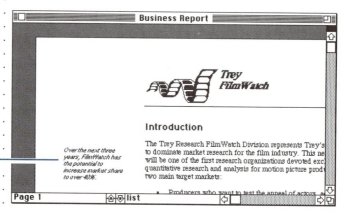

To position selections of text (as this paragraph is positioned in the margin), you'll want to use the Frame command from the Format, not Insert, menu.

narrow margin, or as a caption under a graphic. To do this, you'll use the Format menu's Frame command, which lets you choose the width for the frame you're positioning.

Select the paragraph or paragraphs to position, and then choose Frame from the Format menu (*not* the Insert menu). Type the desired width into the Frame Width box (using the measurement system specified by *Word's* Preferences command—inches, centimeters, whatever else). Then click the Position button, and *Word* switches to its Print Preview mode to give a reduced view of the page. Click on or inside your positioned text's dotted frame, and drag its outline anywhere on the page. When you release the mouse button, *Word* waits a moment and then moves the frame to the point you specified, wrapping any overlapping text around the frame.

Resetting text frame width. If you're not satisfied with the frame's new width, then leave Print Preview and highlight the positioned item. Choose Frame from the Format menu again, and type a new width into the Frame Width box. Then click the Position button to place the item.

Frames with Relative References

When you position a text or graphics frame, that frame stays in its location until you move it again. But sometimes, you'll want to position a frame with a relative reference point such as a margin, a column boundary, or a passage of text. With this approach, the positioned

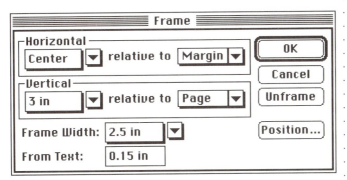

Use the Frame command under the Format menu to align items to relative reference points, like left of a page margin, or center of two columns. You can also enter measurement values (i.e. 2 inches) in the Horizontal and Vertical boxes.

frame will move if its reference point moves—for instance, if you change a page's margins, then a frame that's been positioned in reference to the margins will move to the new margin boundaries. Or if you position a frame relative to a text heading in your document, the frame will follow that heading as it shifts up or down on the page in the course of editing.

To position an item with a relative reference, first select the item and then choose Frame from the Format menu (*not* the Insert menu). By using the Frame dialog box's Horizontal and Vertical options, you can align an item to almost anything, almost anywhere.

Horizontal alignment. Choose the reference that you'll align an item to—either the edges of the entire page, its margins, or just a column inside the margin. Then

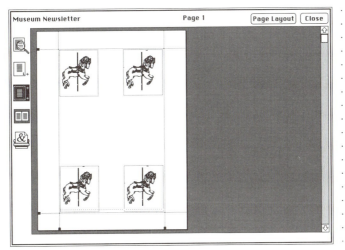

I've aligned these four graphics to the upper left and right margins, and lower left and right margins of the page. Besides margins, Word also lets you align items to page edges, and column boundaries.

Chapter Seven ▾ Miscellaneous Stuff

❗ *You may want to align an item to a horizontal reference point, but align the item vertically to a fixed point (or vice versa). First use the Frame command from the Insert menu to position the item in the fixed horizontal or vertical spot. Then select it again, and use the Format menu's Frame command to align it to the desired relative reference point.*

decide how to align the item to that reference point—you can align it Left, Center, Right, Inside, or Outside to the reference (the Inside and Outside options are for documents that use facing pages with inside and outside margins). Make your alignment and reference point selections with the two buttons under Horizontal in the Frame dialog box. Some possibilities might be to align a graphic Left, relative to the page's Column—this way, if you ever change the column's dimensions, the graphic nonetheless aligns itself with the column's left side. Or to center a graphic between two columns, you'd align it Center, relative to the page's Margin. Click the Position button to see the results.

Vertical alignment. You can align an item either to the Top, Center, or Bottom of your entire page, or just to its margins. Make your alignment and reference point selections with the two buttons under Vertical in the Frame dialog box. Click Position to see the results.

Aligning items to text. You might also want to align an item to text—for instance, align a graphic positioned in the margin to a related heading in your main text. This way, the positioned graphic stays with the text, regardless of editing changes that may shift the text up or down the page, or to a new page altogether. To align an item to text, first insert the item into your document text, directly *above* the paragraph you'd like to align it to. Then select the item, and choose Frame from the

To align an item, such as a graphic, to a text heading, first place the item directly above the heading you'd like to align it to. Then select the item, choose Frame from the Format menu, and choose its horizontal position (it's up to you). The vertical value should be "inline."

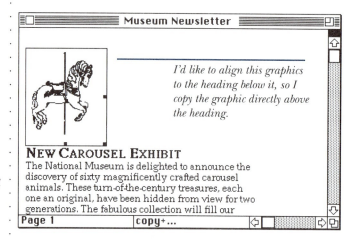

I'd like to align this graphics to the heading below it, so I copy the graphic directly above the heading.

152

Miscellaneous Stuff ▼ CHAPTER SEVEN

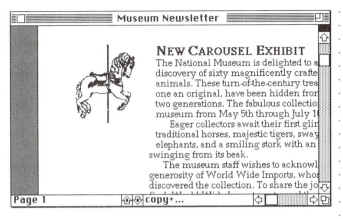

Here the graphic has been aligned to the New Carousel Exhibit heading. The graphic will stick with the heading, even if the heading shifts position during text editing.

Format menu. Select any horizontal reference or value you'd like, and then choose In Line from the Vertical alignment button. This tells *Word* to keep the item in line with the paragraph that followed it. Click the Position button to see if the item is placed correctly. You may have to adjust the item's horizontal positioning to get it in the proper spot.

MAKING VOICE ANNOTATIONS

If your Macintosh has a built-in microphone (as all new models do, since the Mac LC and IIsi), or if you've attached a third-party microphone like Farallon's MacRecorder, then you can record voice annotations in your *Word* documents—a group of editors, for instance, could record comments and suggestions to each other as they jointly work on a manuscript. Once you record an annotation, *Word* uses a speaker symbol to indicate the annotations in your document.

This speaker symbol tells you a voice annotation has been recorded. Double-click the speaker to play the recording.

By the way, while your Mac needs a microphone to record annotations, any Mac can play them back.

Recording Annotations

Position the text cursor wherever you'd like to insert the annotation, and then choose Voice Annotation from the Insert menu to bring up the appropriate dialog box. Click the Record button, lean towards the Mac's micro-

CHAPTER SEVEN ▾ Miscellaneous Stuff

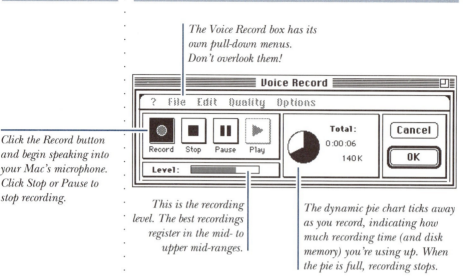

The Voice Record box has its own pull-down menus. Don't overlook them!

Click the Record button and begin speaking into your Mac's microphone. Click Stop or Pause to stop recording.

This is the recording level. The best recordings register in the mid- to upper mid-ranges.

The dynamic pie chart ticks away as you record, indicating how much recording time (and disk memory) you're using up. When the pie is full, recording stops.

💡 *You can move voice annotations within documents by cutting, copying and pasting their respective speaker symbols.*

Quality
✓ Best [0:00:06]
   Better [0:00:19]
   Good [0:00:38]

You can set recording quality from the Quality menu in the Voice Record box. The bracketed times indicate the time limits for each quality level.

phone, and start speaking. Notice the dialog box's Level bar indicates the volume level you're recorded at. Ideally, the level should register between one half and three quarters on the bar. Also notice that your recording time is displayed under Total, and how the pie chart progressively fills to show the time you have left to speak. Click the Stop button when you've finished your annotation. If you'd like to hear it, click the Play button. Use the Cancel button if you don't want to keep the annotation; clicking OK saves the annotation and places its corresponding speaker symbol in your text.

Quick recording. You can also record an annotation directly from your document, without all the dialog box complications. Hit Control-Command-A to start recording, and Command-Period(.) to stop.

Sound quality and recording time. You can adjust the sound quality, and recording time limits for the annotations you record. Before clicking the Record button, pull down the Quality menu in the Voice Annotation dialog box to select Good, Better, and Best options. The better the quality, the less recording time you'll have, however, and each option lists its respective time limit. You can, however, adjust *Word's* default time limits for recording. In the Voice Annotation box, choose Preferences from the Options menu, and type in a new time limit. Longer recordings will use more memory in *Word*, and make your document larger.

Playing Annotations

Position your text cursor just before the annotation's speaker symbol, and then choose Voice Annotations from the View menu—*Word* opens the appropriate dialog box, and moves to the annotation following the text cursor. Click the Play button to listen.

Also, notice the other options available in the Voice Annotations box. Annotator tells which user recorded the annotation (*Word* uses the person's initials set by the Preferences command, under Tools), while Number gives that annotation's sequential rank out of all the annotations in the document. The Next and Previous buttons move you back and forth between annotations in the document, while Find will track down the annotation you specify in the Number box.

💡 *Word formats an annotation's speaker symbol with the Hidden text style, so it doesn't print on paper. If you'd like to hide the symbols on-screen, choose Preferences from the Tools menu, click the View icon, and uncheck the Hidden Text option. You might do this to ensure that line endings and page breaks you see on-screen will appear exactly as they'll print.*

Double-click a speaker icon to play recordings from this Voice Annotations box.

Annotator lists the initials of the person who recorded the voice annotation. You can give Word your proper initials by choosing Preferences from the Tools menu.

To move directly to a particular voice annotation, type it's number into the Number box, and then click the Find button.

Quick playing. You can also play annotations—without all the dialog box options—by holding the Option key, and double-clicking the annotation's speaker symbol.

Chapter Seven ▾ Miscellaneous Stuff

MATH CALCULATIONS

Word's Calculate command lets you add, subtract, multiply, divide, and figure percentages directly in your document. First you select a series of numbers in your text, and then choose Calculate (or Command-Equals (=)) from the Tools menu. *Word* displays the result in the lower left corner of your document window, and also stores the value in the Clipboard, so you can paste it into your text.

Word displays the answer to its calculations in the lower-left corner of your document window.

Adding Columns and Rows

You'll probably use Calculate to add numbers featured in the columns and rows of a table (the table can be created either through *Word's* special Table feature, or with tabbed text). To add table numbers, simply highlight the desired cells or entire columns or rows in the table. To select columns of tabbed figures, hold down the Option button and highlight the desired column. Choose Calculate from the Tools menu, and *Word* displays the addition result in the lower left corner of the document window. By the way, *Word* ignores any text in the data you've highlighted—for instance, "50 feet" would count as "50." Also, *Word* subtracts, rather than adds, any figures that are in parenthesis, such as "(250)", since this is common notation for a loss.

Other Math Functions

To subtract, multiply, divide, or figure percentages, you'll have to type in the desired numbers along with an appropriate math function operator. For instance, "100-50" would indicate 100 minus 50, while "100/50" means 100 divided by 50. Likewise, use the asterisk operator for multiplication (100*50), the percent symbol to figure a percent (495*6.5%), and the plus sign, or a space, for simple addition (45+55, or 45 55).

💡 *Unfortunately, you can't program Word to place math totals in designated cells of a table, and update those totals if their figures ever change. To do this, you'll need to use a spreadsheet like Microsoft Excel or Works.*

Highlight these simple statements in your document, and then choose Calculate from the Tools menu to see *Word's* answer.

By the way, *Word* calculates any values in parenthesis separately from the rest of the math statement. Typing

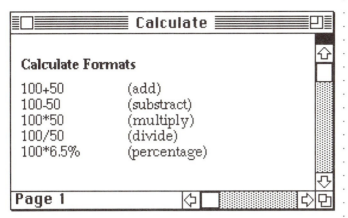

Here are the proper formats for adding, subtracting, multiplying, dividing, and figuring percentages with the Calculate command. Just highlight an equation, and choose Calculate from the Tools menu.

8+(5*4) therefore yields 28, whereas 8+5*4 comes to 52. It doesn't, however, interpret parenthesis as prompts for multiplication, such as "6(6)" to mean "36."

Sorting Information

Use *Word's* Sort feature to arrange paragraphs, tables, and other lists either alphabetically or numerically. For instance, you might want to sort a customer list table by customer's last name, or sort a phone list by area code.

To do a sort, first highlight a range of information, and then choose Sort from the Tools menu. *Word* first arranges the paragraphs, lines, and cells where punctuation marks (!, #, $, %, etc.) come first, numbers come second, then uppercase letters, and finally lowercase. Letters are sorted from A to Z, and numbers from 0 to 9. If you'd like to sort in reverse (Z to A, 9 to 0), hold down the Shift key when you select Sort from the Tools menu.

Sorting table rows. If you're sorting rows in a table, highlight the range of cells in the column you'd like to sort by—for instance, highlight the zip code column to sort by zip. You can also highlight two side by side columns—a last name and first name column, perhaps—and *Word* sorts by the left-most column, and then sorts that column's identical data by the second column. For instance, sorting by last- and first-name columns would

Save your document before doing a sort. That way, if you don't like the sort's results, you always have the original, unsorted information to return to.

Chapter Seven ▼ Miscellaneous Stuff

A before-and-after sort of a simple table-formatted list of names.

Before Sort		After Sort	
Kobler	Helmut	Carlson	David
Macdonald	Leigh	Field	Dan
Little	Ronald	Glennon	Jim
Carlson	David	Kobler	Helmut
Ross	Alan	Li	Eric
Stoiber	Steve	Little	Ronald
Li	Eric	Macdonald	Leigh
Persidsky	Andre	Persidsky	Andre
Glennon	Jim	Ross	Alan
Field	Dan	Stoiber	Steve

produce "Smith, Alan" "Smith, Kathy" and "Smith, Zachary" in that order.

Sorting tabbed data. To sort rows consisting of tabbed columns, hold down the Option key, and highlight the desired column to sort by. Then choose Sort from Tools.

Sorting paragraphs. Your document may call for numbered paragraphs—for instance, a step-by-step checklist—or simple lists of names that you want to sort. Highlight the range of paragraphs to sort, and then choose Sort from Tools.

PRINT MERGE FOR FORM LETTERS AND MAILING LABELS

*Word's Prin*t Merge feature lets you generate form letters and mailing labels. Let me say right now that using the Print Merge is no breeze, but it *is made easier by Word* 5.0's new Print Merge Helper feature. If you've used Print Merge in version 4.0, then you'll be glad to know that by choosing the Print Merge Helper command from the View menu, you can automate the creation of main and data documents, and also insert field names and special merge commands with the handy new Print Merge command bar. By browsing over the next few pages, you'll get a good feel for how the new feature works, and be on your way. And if you're new to print merging altogether, then you're fortunate for starting now, and avoiding much of the clunkyness involved previously.

💡 *To Remove Borders, just select the bordered text, table or picture, choose Border from the Format menu, and click the None icon in the Preset Borders area.*

By the way, this being a Little Book, I'll explain how to do basic, straightforward print merges that are called for in many everyday projects. There's actually a lot more to the feature, however, such as a semiprogramming language that helps make print merging "smarter." Consult your *Word* manual for an exhaustive account of all the print merge details.

Print Merge Basics

Any print merge you do involves two types of documents—the *data document*, and the *main document*. The *data document* contains all the information unique to each instance in the merge—for instance, the various names and addresses that are inserted into a form letter, or the addresses that are printed on mailing labels. The data document is organized, by the way, into *fields*, where each field holds a different type of information. In a mailing list data document, commonplace fields might include customer name, company, address, city, state, and zip code. And a single collection of all the fields is called a *record*. One record would include all the relevant information for, say, a Mrs. Jones, while another record would be for a Mr. Smith.

By the way, you can create your data document in *Word*, or it can come from another application, such as a spreadsheet or database program (see page 161 for more on importing data).

The *main document* is the document that you'll merge all your data into. Here you'll type in the standard text that appears in all instances of the print merge, such as the copy for an invoice, or a past due notice, or an advertisement. You'll also insert references in the places where the form letter should refer to some data field—for instance, "Dear <<first name>> <<last name>>" would call up the two fields that contain a customer's name.

Once you've prepared your main and data documents, you can merge them together with a simple command, and then print out the resulting form letters, mailing labels, etc.

Creating a Data Document

If you're doing a print merge from scratch, it's best to create your data document first. Select New from the File menu to open a new document. Without typing anything, choose the Print Merge Helper command under the View menu. *Word* asks if you'd like to open an existing data document, or start a new one. The new document you just opened is actually going to become your main document, so click the New button here, and *Word* opens its Data Document Building dialog box. In the Field Name box, type the first field for your data, such as "name" or "home address," and click the Add button (by the way, field names can include numbers and multiple words, but not commas). Do the same for any other fields you have, and then click OK when finished. *Word* asks to save your data document, so give it a name, choose a folder to hold the file, and click the Save button.

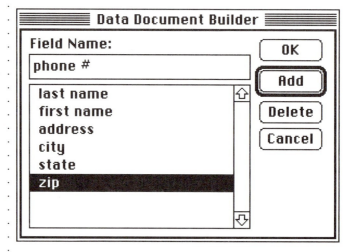

Part of Word's new print merge finesse is that you can create data fields easily through this dialog box (you get here by creating a new data document with the Print Merge Helper command, under View). Just type in the desired field names, and click Add. Word automatically creates a data document based on the fields you've named.

At this point, *Word* takes all the field names you've entered, and creates a table with each field represented by a column in the table. *Word* also switches to the main document you created earlier, and inserts a special DATA instruction that tells the main document where to find its associated data file. Notice also that a new Print Merge Helper command bar appears at the top of your document. I'll explain its functions soon.

last name	first name	address	city	state	zip
Carlson	David	311 Cheesy	Oakland	CA	94716
Field	Dan	16 Funston	San Francisco	CA	94118
Glennon	Jim	6543 Owesalot	Davis	CA	95603
Kobler	Helmut	238 11th Ave.	San Francisco	CA	94118
Li	Eric	69 Getaliphe	Mountain View	CA	94474
Little	Ronald	2738 Parker	Berkeley	CA	94704
Macdonald	Leigh	273 Ichliebedich	Berkeley	CA	94704
Persidsky	Andre	11 59th St.	San Francisco	CA	94119
Ross	Alan	2 Regent	El Cerito	CA	94611
Stoiber	Steve	311 Bowditch	Oakland	CA	94716

Word created this table, based on the data fields I specified in the Data Document Builder box (previous page). I merely had to type the data into the table, hitting Tab to jump from cell to cell.

Entering data. Let's return to the data document, however, by selecting it from the Window menu. Once *Word* creates the table with the specified fields, you're ready to enter all your data inside—again, each column represents a field, and each row represents a single record. Position your text cursor in any cell of the table, and type in a figure, or some other information. You can create multiple lines in a single cell, by the way—for instance, if an address consists of both a street and building name, or perhaps a mail stop. Just make sure that the data you enter is in its respective field column—for instance, customer names should go in the Names column. Use the Tab key to move to the next cell, and Shift-Tab to move backwards a cell. When you get to the last cell in the table (the bottom right-most), hit the Tab key again to create a new row.

❗ *You can use Word's Sort command to sort your data document—for instance, by last name, or zip code—and then print the merged document in this order. See page 157.*

Adding a field to the table. Click the mouse just outside the end of the table's first row of data, so the text cursor sits outside the last cell in the row. Choose Table Layout from the Format menu, check the Column option, and click the Insert button. *Word* creates a new column for you. Note, however, that it doesn't really matter what order your columns are in—they aren't for show, but just so *Word* can differentiate all the data you give it.

Using Data from Other Programs

You may have created data lists in other programs such as Microsoft *Excel*, *FileMaker Pro*, or *Microsoft Works*, and want to merge the information in *Word*. First, keep in mind that these applications may do print merges themselves, and it may be worth exploring their features. If you insist on using *Word*, though, here are the steps for converting outside print merge data. Once you do the

Chapter Seven ▾ Miscellaneous Stuff

> 💡 *If you're using System 7, you can have Word automatically update imported data when that data is changed in its original program (FileMaker or Excel, perhaps). See page 191 for details about Word's Publish and Subscribe feature.*

proper conversions, remember to save your imported data document as a *Word* file. Also, refer to the upcoming section, *Creating a Main Document from an Existing Data Document,* for information on tying the data to a main document.

From Excel. With *Excel,* or another spreadsheet, you can simply highlight the desired columns and rows of data, copy them into the Clipboard, and then paste them into your *Word* document. With *Excel,* at least, the pasted cells will take the form of a table.

From other applications. You'll probably have to bring data into *Word* as a pure text file (also known as ASCII). Each data record becomes a new paragraph, while each record's fields are separated by tabs (sometimes commas). When you bring this information into *Word,* be sure to delete any extra spaces before and after the data rows—extra space may confuse *Word* as it tries to recognize the data.

Adding field headers. You'll have to add field headers to the columns of data you bring in, so *Word* knows which data belongs in which fields. If you've brought in tabbed text, position your text cursor at the beginning of the first row of data, and type in each field header, using tabs or commas to separate each. Then hit Return to move the actual data down to the next line. By the way, it doesn't matter if the headers you create line up with actual columns of data—just make sure they're in the appropriate order, and properly separated.

If your imported data is in *Word's* table format, position your cursor in the first row of cells, and choose Table

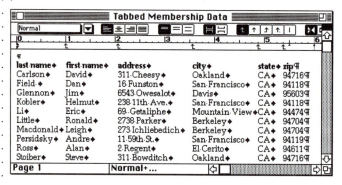

Word will also accept from other sources. Here's a tabbed-text version of some imported data.

Layout from the Format menu. Select the Row option, click the Insert button, and *Word* inserts a new row on top. Now enter the appropriate field names.

Creating the Main Document

If you followed the steps in *Creating a Data Document* above, then you've already also created your main document—it was the new document you opened at the very start, where *Word* inserted its special DATA command when you created your data fields. If you created a data document earlier, or imported it from another source, then refer to the next section, *Creating a Main Document from an Existing Data Document.*

For the former case, however, select this document from *Word's* Window menu (or open it, if it's not already available), and then enter all the standard text you'd like. You can format the text just like you would with any other *Word* document. Make sure you don't insert anything before the DATA command, however.

Inserting field references. When you want to insert data from the data document, choose the appropriate field name from the Insert Field Name button on the Print Merge Helper command bar. *Word* inserts the field name, and encloses it with open and closed print merge

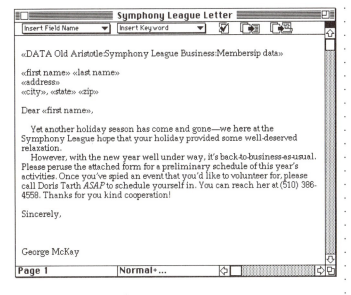

Here's a sample main document. Notice the DATA statement at the top, which tells Word where to find the corresponding data document that will merge with this form letter. Also notice the Print Merge Helper command bar at the top of the window. You can click the Insert Field Name button to quickly plug in data field names into your main document.

Chapter Seven ▾ Miscellaneous Stuff

> ❗ *Instead of using the Print Merge helper command bar, you can manually type data field names into a main document, but don't use your keyboard's < and > characters to indicate the field's open and closed brackets. Press Option-\ for an open bracket symbol, then type the field name, and press Shift-Option-\ for a closed bracket.*

brackets. For instance, part of your form letter might read "<<first name>> <<last name>>! *You may have just won $500,000,000!!!*" You can also highlight these references and apply all of *Word's* standard formatting (font, size, style, etc.). You're now ready to merge the main document with its data.

Creating a Main Document from an Existing Data Document

If you've created a data document on an earlier occasion, use this approach to create its corresponding main document. Start a new *Word* document, or open one where you've already typed in all the standard text to be print merged. This document will become the main document.

Position your text cursor at the beginning of the very first line of the document, making sure that no characters precede the cursor. Choose Print Merge Helper from the View menu—*Word* responds with a dialog box, and asks if you'd like to open or create a new data document. Choose the existing data document from the file list, and click the Open button. *Word* inserts its special DATA command at the top of your new main document, and notes all the existing fields in the data document you just selected. Format the main document as you'd like, and insert field references by positioning the cursor in the appropriate spot, and choosing a field from the Insert Field Name button on the Print Merge Helper command bar. You're now ready to merge the main document with its data.

> ❗ *If Word isn't displaying the Print Merge Helper command bar, you can turn it on by selecting Print Merge from the File menu, and click the Show Helper button.*

Merging Documents

When merging your main and data documents, you can choose whether to merge and print the documents, or merge and save them to disk. This is done by clicking the appropriate icons on the Print Merge Helper bar, if it's displayed, or by choosing the Print Merge Helper bar from the File menu. Using the Print Merge command from File gives you added flexibility, by the way, in that you can specify a range of records to merge. Using the icons on the command bar merges *all* the records.

Miscellaneous Stuff ▼ **CHAPTER SEVEN**

You can choose Print Merge from the File menu to call up the Print Merge dialog box, or click the three icons on the Print Merge Helper command bar to select your merge options.

To merge with either method, make sure that your main document is open, and that it contains the DATA command that identifies its related data document. Choose Print Merge from the File menu, and check either the Merge and Print or Merge and Save options (*or*, as I said, you can simply click the corresponding icons on the Print Merge Helper bar). If you want to specify a range of records, type the first record number in the From box, and the last in the To box. Then click the OK button to go ahead with the merge.

Click this icon on the Print Merge Helper command bar to check your main and data documents for possible merge errors.

Merge and Print. This calls up the familiar Print dialog box, where you can specify various options related to the type of paper you're feeding to the printer, and so on.

Click these icons to save your print merge document to disk, or to print the document.

Merge and Save. This saves all the merged documents in another big document called "Merge1." You can open this file to inspect the results, and apply any extra formatting or other changes.

Only Check for Errors. *Word* scans your main and data documents, and report any problems, such as missing field characters, or unrecognized fields.

Continuing merging after a problem. Sometimes your print merge may be interrupted by a problem with your printer—a paper jam, most likely. To continue the merge, note (or approximate) the last record printed, and then use the Print Merge command from the File menu to specify a range starting at that record.

165

CHAPTER SEVEN ▾ Miscellaneous Stuff

MERGING MAILING LABELS

Merging and printing data on mailing labels is an involved task, since it requires special page setup options for printers. It also means specially designing your main document so that data fields appear within the boundaries of the mailing labels. What's more, this all depends on if you're using an ImageWriter or LaserWriter printer, as well as the number of columns on your label sheets. Explaining this from scratch could take up a Little Book all by itself, but fortunately, Microsoft provides preformatted label files which you can easily adapt to your own projects. You'll find these files in the Mailing Labels folder in *Word's* Sample Documents folder. Many files are included for both laser and dot matrix printers, as well as for the label formats you're using (two or three columns, 12 or 24 labels per page, etc.). To help decide which label file to use, first read the Mailing Labels ReadMe file in the Mailing Labels folder.

These files have all the appropriate page setup and margin settings that standard labels require, and are designed with special IF... and ENDIF... statements to avoid printing blank lines when a certain data field—such as company name—is empty for a particular record.

Adjustments to make. You'll have to make a few changes to *Word's* predesigned mailing label documents. First, you'll have to replace the field names used by Microsoft with whatever actual field names you use in your data document. Just highlight the field names in the Microsoft document, and type in the names for your corresponding field—be sure not to remove any of the surrounding brackets, however. Depending on the size

Mailing Labels ReadMe

Be sure to read this file before using one of Word's preformatted mailing label files. It's in the Mailing Labels folder in the Sample Documents folder.

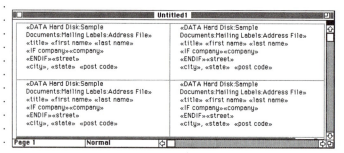

You'll have to plug in your own DATA statement (corresponding to the name and location of your data document), and custom data field names before using one of Word's preformatted mailing label files.

of the labels you're using, you may also have to adjust the height and width of the file's label sizes to match your own. This is a trial and error process that could require a few test prints to fine-tune. Also make sure to insert a DATA statement that refers *Word* to your corresponding data document—position your cursor at the very top of the main document, and then follow the steps in the earlier section, *Creating a Main Document from an Existing Data Document*.

Merging and Printing Labels

Once you've set up your main document for labels, make sure to properly feed the labels into your printer. For ImageWriters, adjust the print head and set the form feed so the printing starts at the top of the first row of labels. On LaserWriters, you'll probably insert the label sheets into your paper cassette.

Now follow the steps in the *Merging Documents* section above. Before printing on labels, however, you may want to print a test sheet or two on regular paper, and make sure all the spacing and margins fit on the label sheets.

MATH AND SCIENTIFIC EQUATIONS

Formatting scientific equations in earlier versions of *Word* used to be like pulling teeth. You'd sit hunched at your Mac, *Word's* tome-like reference manual open in your lap, and look up archaic codes corresponding to the math expressions and symbols you wanted to typeset. Once you had typed in the proper codes, you'd preview your work on-screen—more often then not, the result required a good half-hour of fine tuning.

Word still supports these code-based equations, in case you'd like to use your old ones from earlier versions of the program, or simply if you have sadistic tendencies, and *enjoy* struggling with those horrid codes. For the rest of us, however, *Word's* new Equation Editor takes a far more easier, visual approach to equation building. You simply pick prebuilt expressions on screen, and then plug in whatever numbers, symbols or text you'd like.

Chapter Seven ▾ Miscellaneous Stuff

Using the Equation Editor with System 6 and 7. How you use *Word's* equation editor depends on if your Mac is running System 6 or System 7. For System 6, then you'll use the Equation Editor as a stand-alone program, separate from the *Word*. To do this, double-click the Equation Editor file in your Word Commands folder. When you've finished creating an equation in the program, you'll copy and paste the equation into *Word* via the Mac's Clipboard (see page 188 for more about copying and pasting). If you're using System 7, however, you can use the Equation Editor directly within *Word*—choose Object from the Insert menu, select the Equation option from the Object Type box that appears, and then click OK. *Word* opens the Equation Editor window for you; when you're finished building the equation, just close the window and the equation automatically appears in your *Word* document.

Starting an Equation

When you open the Equation Editor, you're faced with an empty window in which you'll assemble equations. Above the window, notice the palettes of symbols and equation icons—click these to insert the appropriate math symbols and equations into the window. Notice particularly the Template equations along the bottom row of palettes—these are standard, predesigned expressions that find their way into regular, everyday work—for

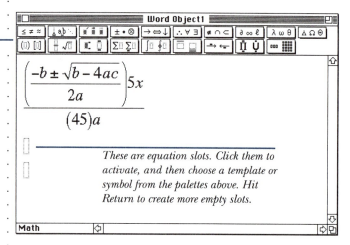

The Symbol and Template palettes. Click each palette to see the various forms available.

instance, a square root, a radical, or a matrix. Pick the appropriate template, and *Word* displays it on screen.

Plugging in numbers and text. The templates you insert on-screen feature their appropriate symbols, signs or expressions (for instance, a square root sign) but they also include dotted empty boxes, which hold the text or numbers that you'll plug into your equation. To insert these elements, just click the desired dotted box, and then type in your entry—for instance, in the square root sign, you might type "64+16."

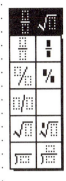

One of the Equation Editor's many template palettes. Just pick the expression that's right for you, and Word inserts it into the equation window.

This square root template features two empty slots. You can click a slot, and then enter a value or text.

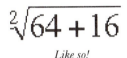

Like so!

$\dfrac{25}{5}$ *How you add elements to an expression depends on where you place the text cursor in the expression. Notice how the cursor on the left expression only spans the "25"—anything you type will be added to the numerator slot of the fraction, since that's where the cursor is. On the other hand, in the expression on the right, anything typed will be added next to the entire fraction, since that's what the cursor spans.* $\dfrac{25}{5}|$

Tips for Creating Complex Equations

If you're only creating simple equations, such as plain fractions and square roots, then you'll get the hang of things almost immediately. On the other hand, your work may call for more complex structures—equations within equations within equations (the stuff that scared us all to death in high school). Fortunately, you can format intimidating equations by creating them one element at a time, and then combining those finished,

> By default, the Equation Editor shows your equations at two times their actual size (so they're more legible as you build them). To see them at true size, and other magnifications, pull down the View menu and make the desired selection.

CHAPTER SEVEN ▾ Miscellaneous Stuff

> *You can get online help for Word's Equation Editor by pulling down the Apple menu, choosing About Equation Editor, and then clicking the box's Help button.*

independent elements into a single equation. This may sound convoluted at first, but take a look at the equation in the document window on page 168. I actually put that together in about a minute. First, I created the -b± square root numerator, and then, in another slot, chose a fraction template. I highlighted the first expression with the mouse, and chose Cut from the Equation Editor's Edit menu. Then I clicked the numerator slot of the fraction I just created, and chose Paste from the Edit menu. By those simple steps, I moved one expression into another. You'll get the hang of it within minutes.

CHAPTER 8

Printing Your Documents

What's Inside

- ▼ Setting Up Your Printer
- ▼ Printing Basics
- ▼ Setting Up Pages for Printing
- ▼ Printing with Different Printers
- ▼ Printing Envelopes
- ▼ Printing PostScript Disk Files
- ▼ Printing Linked Documents

Chapter Eight ▾ Printing Your Documents

Printing *Word* documents is usually just a matter of telling *Word* which pages to print, and then waiting for your Mac's printer to churn out the pages. Nonetheless, *Word* supports various other options and secondary features that will be useful to know about as well. I'll talk here about *Word's* various printing talents, from the basics to printing envelopes to saving PostScript files to configuring *Word* to work best with your particular printer. I start with *Printing Basics*, since this topic offers the bulk of what everyone needs to know. Also, if you plan to print drafts of your document with one kind of printer, like an ImageWriter, and then print final pages with a different model, like a LaserWriter, then be sure to read the section, *Printing with Different Printers*, on page 180. If you're not careful, certain problems may arise.

SETTING UP YOUR PRINTER

Before tackling any printing issues, let's make sure that you've already hooked up your printer, and that it's ready to go. If this isn't the case, then this little bit of information will probably be helpful to you: besides physically attaching the printer to your Macintosh, you've also got to install special software, called a "printer driver," in your Mac's System Folder. The printer driver gives your Mac some particular information about the printer it's hooked up to, and each printer model has its own unique driver—for instance, there's a LaserWriter driver, an ImageWriter driver, a StyleWriter driver, and so on.

LaserWriter

StyleWriter

Here are the printer driver file icons for LaserWriter and StyleWriter printers.

Your printer should have come with a driver disk, or you can find drivers for many popular models on the System disks that came with your Macintosh. Either way, to install the printer driver file, simply copy it into your Mac's System Folder (or the System Folder's Extensions folder if you're using Apple's System 7 software).

Choosing with the Chooser. You're almost done, but not quite. With the printer driver in your System Folder, you've now got to select it. Choose Chooser from under your Mac's Apple menu. This calls up the Chooser

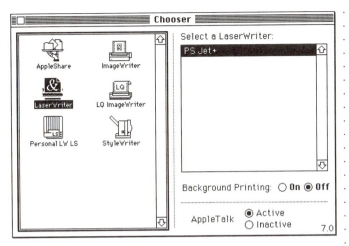

Use the Apple menu's Chooser to select the printer you'd like to use with Word. Here I've picked the LaserWriter printer driver from a number of different printer types.

window, which displays all the printer drivers installed in your Mac. Click the driver for your particular printer. For LaserWriters, the Chooser will also ask you to click on the name of your LaserWriter; for ImageWriters and other printers, you'll have to specify the Mac port that the printer is hooked into (chances are, it's your Mac's printer port). When you've made the appropriate selections, just close the Chooser window, and you're ready to print with *Word*.

PRINTING BASICS

To print a document, first make sure it's open and that its document window is active. Choose Print from the File menu (or type Command-P), and *Word* calls up its Print dialog box. The dialog box looks different depending on whether you're using a LaserWriter and StyleWriter printer or an ImageWriter, but your basic options are the same. You'll be able to set a number of print options, and then click the Print button (or OK in some cases) to send the document through.

Choosing What to Print

Ordinarily, *Word* prints all of the pages in your document from first to last. However, you can also specify a limited page range, by typing the first page to print into the

From box, and the last page of the range into To (hit the Tab key to move the cursor to these boxes without using the mouse). If you've created sections in your document (see page 72 for details about these), you can also give *Word* a range of sections to print. By entering values in both the Pages and Section Range boxes, *Word* can start printing a section at a specified page, and end the range at another page in a different section—for instance, a page range of 5–10, and a section range of 3–5 would print from page 5 in section 3, to page 10 of section 5.

Printing a selection of text. To print a selection of text without specifying a page range, first highlight the selection, call up the Print dialog box, and check the Print Selection Only option. Then click the Print button (or OK).

Printing multiple documents. To print multiple documents at once, quit *Word* and return to the Mac's Finder (otherwise known as the "Desktop"). Place the desired document files in a single folder (if they're not already in the same folder), and then select all the files as a group—either choose Select All from Finder's Edit menu, or click each file while holding down the Shift key. Choose Print from the Finder's File menu to load *Word*, and call up its Print dialog box. Select any print options you'd like, and then click the Print button (or OK).

Other Print Options

Here's a rundown of the various options offered in the Print dialog box. Some of these are common to both LaserWriter and ImageWriter printers, while others are exclusive to one model. By the way, I'm concentrating on

Here's the Print dialog box for LaserWriter printers. Notice all the print options available.

the options available to standard LaserWriters (and compatibles) and ImageWriters because these are the most popular printers used on the Mac. If you have another printer, such as Apple's ImageWriter LQ, StyleWriter, or Personal LaserWriter LS, then your printer options will vary slightly from the ones described here. Not to worry, however. The differences are usually quite minor, so you can easily figure out your own printer's options by reading up on the ones here.

Universal options. In *Copies*, you can tell *Word* to print from 1 to 999 copies of a whole document or a page range. For *Paper Source*, choose Paper Cassette for LaserWriters, or Automatic for ImageWriters, to have paper feed to the printer automatically. Choose Manual Feed, or Hand Feed for ImageWriters, to manually feed custom page sizes, envelopes, or, for the ImageWriter, individual sheets to the printer. *Print Hidden Text* prints all text formatted in the Hidden character style (see page 55 for more about the Hidden style). Use this option to print table of contents and index entry codes, or to show commentary that you might have formatted as Hidden. Otherwise, this option should be kept off. Select *Print Next File* if the current file is part of a series of documents—see page 185 for more details.

LaserWriter-specific options. *Cover Page* prints a cover page for your document, giving the document's file name, the time of printing, and a few other details. You can print the cover page at the beginning or end of the document. *Print Back to Front* starts printing from the last page to the first. Depending on your printer, you may have to use this option so that pages print in their proper order, with the first page on top and facing up. *Print* lets you choose either *Black and White* for standard printers, or *Color/Grayscale* for printing color text and graphics on a color printer. And *Destination* lets you direct *Word's* output to either your printer, which is standard, or a PostScript file. See page 184 for more details on printing to PostScript.

ImageWriter-specific options. *Quality* lets you specify how your ImageWriter prints text: *Best* prints the darkest and smoothest by printing everything twice over, and at a

> Before printing, it's a good idea to check your document in Word's Page Layout view (under the View menu), or Print Preview (under File). These features show exactly how your pages print on paper, with multiple columns, page numbers, headers and footers, and footnotes.

> Do your documents print backwards, so you constantly have to reshuffle pages? You can fix this, so the first page of your document comes out on top of the page stack, face up. Choose Print from the File menu, and check Word's Print Back to Front option.

Print options for ImageWriters are a little more limited. Most important, however, are the Quality settings, which determine how good printed text and graphics look.

```
ImageWriter                                        7.0      [ Print ]
Quality:     ○ Best        ● Faster     ○ Draft
Page Range:  ○ All         ● From: 5    To: 10            [ Cancel ]
Copies:      1
Paper Feed:  ● Automatic   ○ Hand Feed
Section Range: From: 2     To: 3        ☐ Print Selection Only
☐ Print Hidden Text   ☐ Print Next File
```

slow pace; *Faster* prints text only once, and loses quality accordingly; *Draft* is your fastest option, but this mode prints text without specific font or style formatting.

SETTING UP PAGES FOR PRINTING

Choose Page Setup from the File menu to control other printing settings, such as the paper size you're using, vertical or horizontal page orientations, the margins of your document, special effects and more. You won't always need to use Page Setup, since its default settings are tuned for typical, everyday printing needs. But in other cases you will—for instance, if you're printing your document on a different printer than it was originally composed for. See page 180 for more about this.

By the way, Page Setup options are different for LaserWriters and ImageWriter printers, so I'll explain each separately. If you have yet another printer model, then the your Page Setup options will probably vary slightly from the ones described here, but not by much. You can still learn your way around the Page Setup feature by reading the information here.

General Page Setup Options

Page Setup lets you choose the type of paper you'll be printing on—for LaserWriters, the default is the standard 8.5 by 11 inches Letter size, but you can also pick Legal (8.5 by 14 inches), A4 Letter (European standard, 21 by 29.7 cm.), B5 Letter (17.6 by 25 cm.), Tabloid (11 by 17 inches), and Standard US Business Envelope. For ImageWriter printers, your options are US Letter, Legal, A4 Letter, International Fanfold (8.25 by 12 inches) and Computer Paper (14 by 11 inches).

Setting a custom page size. You can also set up a custom page size by choosing Preferences from the Tools menu. Type your width and height dimensions into the value boxes, and then close the Preferences box. Go back to Page Setup to see your custom measurements listed.

Page orientation. Ordinarily, *Word* prints your document in Portrait mode, so that the reader holds a page vertically to read. You can, however, print in Landscape mode, and *Word* will print horizontally across the wider dimension of the page.

Page margins. You can also set your document's margins by clicking the Document button in the Page Setup box. This brings you to *Word's* Document dialog box, which I explain further on page 74.

Making default settings. Ordinarily, the page size and orientation you set only to the document you're working on. To have your settings apply to all new *Word* documents, check the Use as Default option.

LaserWriter-Specific Options

Here's a rundown of the Page Setup options specifically for LaserWriter and compatible printers.

Reduce or Enlarge. This tells *Word* to print your pages—text, graphics, margins, and so on—at anywhere from 25 to 400 percent of their regular size. You'd do this to fit more or less information on a particular page.

Font Substitution. Sometimes you might format your documents in a font that the LaserWriter can't print very clearly. These "bit-mapped" fonts are usually named after cities, like New York, Geneva, or Monaco. Checking the Font Substitution option tells *Word* to substitute any bit-

The LaserWriter Page Setup box. You can click the Options button for even more settings.

mapped fonts in your document with built-in printer fonts that look better—*Word* substitutes New York and other serifed fonts with the printer's Times, Geneva with Helvetica, and Monaco with Courier. Unless you want bit-mapped fonts to print in your document, keep this option checked.

Text and Graphics Smoothing. These two options "blur" the rough edges of bit-mapped text and graphics (such as *MacPaint* pictures), making them appear smoother, but also slowing your printer down. If you're using bit-maps in your documents, experiment with these options on and off to see if they improve anything. If bit-maps don't play a part, turn the options off.

Faster Bitmap Printing. This helps print bit-mapped graphics quicker, but ties up more of your printer's memory intended for printing other graphics and fonts. Use it only if you've got a lot of bit-maps in your document.

Fractional Widths. Your document probably uses proportionally-spaced fonts—these are the most common fonts used by the Mac, where each font's character takes up a different amount of space—an "i" takes less than an "m," for instance. Only a few fonts, like Courier or Monaco are not proportionally spaced—each character, whether a fat "W" or a thin "l" takes the same space on a line.

At any rate, your Mac's screen is not precise enough to show the exact, fine spacing of proportionally-spaced characters. On some occasions, this means that the line endings on your screen don't coincide with what *Word* actually prints—for instance, a line on-screen may end with one word, but when you print, the line ends at a different word. Checking the Fractional Widths option guards against the problem, so the line endings you see on-screen are exactly how they'll print on paper. But this option also causes the text on your screen to be hard to read, since the screen is trying to match the precise spacing of the font. It's better to write your document with this option off, and then turn it on before finally proofing and printing.

> 🛑 *Does your LaserWriter cut off text and graphics at the edges of a page, no matter what margins you set? Choose Page Setup from the File menu, click the Options button, and turn the Larger Print Area option on.*

Print PostScript Over Text. If you have PostScript graphics overlapping any fonts or other graphics in your document, this option prints the PostScript on top, instead of under the text and graphics.

The Options button. Click this button to set some other LaserWriter options. *Flip Horizontal and Vertical* flips your page image left to right, and top to bottom respectively, while Invert image prints pages as negatives—white space is printed black, while text and graphics become white. *Precision Bitmap Alignment* means that *Word* prints bit-mapped graphics (from *MacPaint*, for instance) without their usual tiny distortion, but reduces the size of your page by 4%. I find this option isn't very useful in the long run. Click *Larger Print Area* when you want text and graphics to print as close to the page's edge as possible—ordinarily, *Word* prints a half inch to the edge, but this option reduces that to a quarter inch. Selecting the larger print area, however, will use up some of your printer's memory usually reserved for holding downloaded fonts. These are the fonts that aren't built-in to the printer, but that you've purchased from companies like Adobe or Bitstream, and have installed in your Mac. If your document uses more than five or six of these add-on fonts, and you choose the larger print area, then your printer may slow down a bit to handle both items. And speaking of downloadable fonts—if your document calls for several, then check *Unlimited Downloadable Fonts* to use more printer memory to store them, and increase your printing speed by a bit.

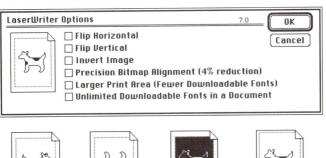

The LaserWriter Options box. Click an option, and the little dog graphic will demonstrate that option's effect on your page.

Flip Horizontal   *Flip Vertical*   *Invert Image*   *Larger Print Area*

This is the Page Setup box you'll see if you use an ImageWriter or most other printer models from Apple.

ImageWriter-Specific Options

If you're using an ImageWriter, you have many fewer Page Setup options to worry about.

Tall Adjusted. Sometimes ImageWriters print graphics with a horizontal distortion, making them seem stretched. Check this option if you're having this problem. Also check it if you plan to eventually print your document on a LaserWriter—this guarantees that the line endings and page breaks you see on-screen will match the LaserWriter's.

50% Reduction. This options prints all the elements on your pages at half-size, to fit more information on each page. To coincide with this reduction, *Word* also doubles the measurements on its Ruler, or in Page Layout or Print Preview views.

No Gaps Between Pages. This option prints pages continuously, with no top or bottom margins. You'll want to check it if you're printing mailing labels, or other forms.

PRINTING WITH DIFFERENT PRINTERS

This is important! *Word* specially formats your documents according to the printer that you're currently using—more specifically, it formats documents according to the printer you've selected with the Mac's Chooser desk accessory, which is listed under the Apple menu. Some elements of your document, in fact, can vary depending on the printer selected—for instance, *Word* spaces the *same* font *differently*, depending on whether you're printing on an ImageWriter or a LaserWriter.

This isn't a problem if you'll always print your documents on the same printer that you've selected in the Chooser. It *is* a problem if you switch printers at some point. For instance, a common scenario is to use a printer like the ImageWriter to draft your documents, but then bring a disk to a computer service bureau to print out on a sleeker LaserWriter. But switching printers like this can raise havoc, so that the line endings, page breaks and the page count in your document turns out differently from one printer to the next. Sometimes the differences will be inconsequential, and you can ignore them (if you even noticed them in the first place). On the other hand, it's bad news if you've spent time fine tuning the pagination of your document, only to find it completely changed.

> *If you're printing your document on a different Macintosh than you created it on—perhaps a Mac at a service bureau—then be sure that the new system has all your document's fonts installed.*

Avoiding Printer Confusion

There are a couple of things you can do to avoid these surprises. Ideally, if you know you'll ultimately print your final documents from a particular printer—for instance, the LaserWriter at the service bureau—then select the LaserWriter printer driver with the Apple menu's Chooser before even starting the document. Do this even if you don't have a LaserWriter on hand at the time. All you're doing is ensuring that the line endings and page breaks you see on-screen will match what you'll get with the printer you've chosen.

If you can't use this foresight, however, there's another option. When you're about to print with a different printer than you've prepared your document for, choose Page Setup from the File menu, and then click OK. *Word* reformats your document to reflect the new printer's settings, and will probably change some of the line endings and page breaks in your document. Browse through the document on-screen to see that everything is okay. If so, you're ready to print with no surprises.

> *If you're preparing your document on an ImageWriter, but plan to finally print on a LaserWriter, then choose Page Setup from the File menu, and check the Tall Adjusted option. This ensures that on-screen line endings and page breaks match those of the LaserWriter.*

Printing Envelopes

Printing envelopes with *Word* is fairly straightforward—first, you type an addressee and, if you like, a return sender address, into a new document. Then format the document's margins to fit a standard US envelope (9.5 by 4 inches)—these margins, however, depend on the kind of printer you're using, and I give a variety of printer settings in the table below. The last step is to feed your envelope into the printer.

Addressing the Envelope

Open a new document by selecting New from *Word's* File menu. If you don't want to print a return address on your envelope, then type the addressee name, putting each address item (such as name, company, and address) on a separate line. If you *do* want to print a return address, start the new document by typing that address first. Following the return address, hit Return about six times to create the space between the return address and addressee areas. With the text cursor positioned on the last line, turn *Word's* Ruler on, and drag its left indent marker to the 3.5 inch mark. Now type in the addressee information, putting each address item on a new line.

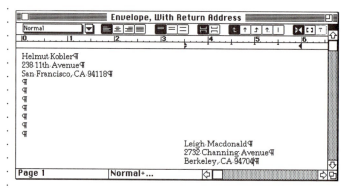

This window shows how to format an envelope with a return address. Remember to use the Ruler to indent the addressee information.

Choose Page Setup from the File menu and select an envelope style for your page size. For some printers, like LaserWriters, you'll choose an envelope type according to how you'd like to feed the envelope into the printer's manual feed guide—choose either Centered, or Edge Fed, so the envelope is aligned with the edge of the manual feed guide. For ImageWriters, choose US Letter, and make sure the No Gaps Between Pages option is off. Finally, choose Landscape Orientation (Portrait for StyleWriter printers).

In the Page Setup box, click the Document button to call up *Word's* Document dialog box. Now type the appropriate margin values for your particular printer—see the next section. Hit OK to leave the Document and Page Setup boxes. Next, choose Print Preview from the File menu to preview the margins of your envelope, and make sure the envelope address information you typed is showing properly. You can drag the page's margin guides to make any necessary adjustments.

Feeding envelopes to a LaserWriter. Finally, you'll have to feed your envelope into the printer. Old LaserWriters use the edge-fed method, where you align the top, left-hand corner of the envelope (face up, by the way) with the edge of the manual feed guide. LaserWriters like the NT, NTX, and SC also can use the center-fed approach, where you'll center the envelope in your printer's sliding manual feed guides (face down). However you feed the envelope, choose Print from the File menu, turn the Manual Feed option on, and click the Print button.

Feeding envelopes to an ImageWriter. For ImageWriters, place the envelope face down into your printer's paper feed, with the envelope flap folded out to the right side. Align the envelope's bottom with the ImageWriter's manual feed guide, and then press the form feed button on your printer to feed the envelope in. Choose Print from the File menu, turn the Hand Feed option on, and click the Print button.

Envelope Margins for Your Printer

Here are the top, bottom, left, right margins to use when printing envelopes on a variety of Apple printers and compatibles. Notice that the margins depend on whether you're printing a return address or not. Understand also that these margins may not be exact, and that you may want to fine-tune them to print your envelopes perfectly.

For LaserWriters and ImageWriters, make sure to set your page orientation to Landscape mode.

Word includes preformatted envelope templates for many popular printers. You can forgo formatting envelope documents and setting margins—all you have to do is plug in your address information and print. Check the Envelopes folder in Word's Sample Documents folder.

Printer	With Return Address		Without	
LaserWriter & Plus	(T).5"	(B)4.75"	(T)1.75"	(B)4.75"
	(L).5"	(R)2"	(L)3.5"	(R)2"
Personal LaserWriter & StyleWriter	(All Margins).5"		(T).1.75"	(B).5"
			(L)3.5"	(R).5"
LaserWriter II and SC	(T)4.5"	(B).5"	(T)5.75"	(B).5"
(edge-fed)	(L).5"	(R)2"	(L)3.5"	(R)2"
(center-fed)	(T)2.5"	(B)2"	(T)4"	(B)=2"
	(L).5"	(R).5"	(L)3.5"	(R).5"
ImageWriter II	(T).5"	(B).5"	(T)2"	(B)1"
	(L).5"	(R)2"	(L)4"	(R)1"

PRINTING POSTSCRIPT DISK FILES

Instead of printing a document to paper, you can "print" it as a PostScript file on disk, where the file contains all the PostScript instructions that describe the document (PostScript, by the way, is a printer language that's used by many popular models, like the LaserWriter II NT). You'll still need a PostScript printer to print the file, but the benefit of this approach is that you can print the file at a computer service bureau, or from another Macintosh that might not have *Microsoft Word* installed. If *Word* isn't on hand, you can use a standard PostScript downloading utility such as Adobe's *SendPS*, or CE Software's *LaserStatus* to load the PostScript *Word* file into the printer.

Printing to Disk

To print PostScript to disk, you need a LaserWriter printer driver installed in your Macintosh (even if you don't own a LaserWriter). The driver should be included on one of your System disks that came with your Macintosh. Put the LaserWriter driver in your System folder (or with System 7, put the file in the Extensions folder) and then use the Mac's Chooser (under the Apple menu) to select the LaserWriter icon. While you're in the Chooser, make sure that Background Printing is turned off.

Next, choose Print from *Word's* File menu, and check any print options you'd like, or pick a page range. If your LaserWriter printer driver is a more recent version, then you'll be able to check the PostScript File option, and then click the Save button. *Word* asks you for a file name, and then prints your PostScript file to disk.

If you don't see a PostScript File option in the Print dialog box, then you've installed an older LaserWriter driver. In this case, click the OK button to start printing, but type Command-K immediately afterward. *Word* creates your PostScript file under the name *POST-SCRIPT0, POSTSCRIPT1*, etc., and places it in your *Word* folder (look in the main directory of your hard disk if it's not in the *Word* folder).

LaserWriter

Make sure that this printer driver is in your System Folder before printing a document as a PostScript file.

Printing Linked Documents

A handy feature of *Word*—especially if you're working with long documents—is that it can link a series of separate files, and then print them as a single document with continuous page numbers.

I explain how to link documents on page 144. To print them, just open any document in the linked chain. Choose Print from the File menu, and check the Print Next File option. If you'd like to print the whole chain, make sure that All is checked in the Pages area.

Printing a page range. If you'd like to print a page range in the *first* document of a linked series, then open that document, choose Print from File, and type in the desired page range. It's more complicated, however, when you want to print a page range in a document that's not first in the linked series. The problem is that *Word* doesn't sequentially number the page numbers of linked documents until it's actually printing and processing those documents. Before then, each linked document thinks that its numbers start at 1. To print a page range from one of those documents—and to ensure that the pages print with the proper page numbers in the linked series—then you'll have to figure out how many pages in other linked documents come before the pages you'd like to print. To do this, count all the pages contained in the documents that are linked *before* the document you'd like to print from. For instance, you might count 100 pages—40 in the first document, 30 in the second document, and 30 in the third. Suppose you'd like to print from the fourth document in the series—you'll have to tell that document that its first page starts at 101, rather than 1.

Here are the steps to take: open the document you'd like to print from, choose Document from the Format menu, and click the File Series button. *Word* produces another dialog box—in its Number From box, type in the number for the first page in this document (remember, it all depends on how many pages precede it in the earlier documents in the series). Click OK to return to *Word's* main menu, and then choose Repaginate Now from the Tools menu to update the page numbers in your document. Now use Print Preview or Page Layout view to note the numbers of the pages you'd like to print. Choose the Print command, uncheck the Print Next File option, and give *Word* the page range you'd like to print. Then click Print.

Use the File Series box to set the starting page number for a linked document.

After printing, you'll want to put the document back in the file series—choose Document again, click the File Series button, and set the Number From box to 0.

An easier compromise. To avoid the hassle above, you can print a page range from a linked document and simply forgo accurate page numbers that reflect the document's sequential order in its series. This is fine if you just want to proofread the pages' text, for instance. To print a range without accurate page numbers, just follow the normal procedure.

CHAPTER 9

Sharing Information with Other Programs

What's Inside

- Sharing Information the Easy Way
- Publishing and Subscribing
- Linking Documents with Other Programs
- Embedding Information
- Linking Information with System 6
- Opening and Saving Documents in Other File Formats
- Placing Word Documents in Other Programs

Some of your *Word* documents may depend on other software. For instance, you might want to incorporate graphics created in *Adobe Illustrator*, or spreadsheet data from an application like *Excel*. Perhaps you'll need to save your *Word* documents in different file formats, so they're compatible with word processors like *MacWrite II* or even *WordPerfect* for the IBM PC. I'll discuss these and related issues here.

Power sharing. Much of this chapter, by the way, covers *Word's* powerful information-sharing talents, such as the Publish and Subscribe feature available on Macs using Apple's System 7 operating system. *Word's* Publish and Subscribe feature is designed for incorporating data into your documents, and then automatically updating that incorporated data if it changes. For instance, you might bring in business figures from an *Excel* spreadsheet. But if someone updates that spreadsheet with new sales figures, you won't have to copy the new data from *Excel* again—*Word* handles all that for you. See the section *Publishing and Subscribing* for the details.

SHARING INFORMATION THE EASY WAY

The easiest way to share information with other programs—for instance, to bring in data or graphics from another application, or to move *Word* text into another program—is to use the straightforward Cut, Copy and Paste commands. If you have even a little Mac experience, you're probably already familiar with the necessary steps, since they work the same in all Macintosh applications. I'll review them here nonetheless.

But before you commit to taking this easy approach to sharing information, you should read up on *Word's* other features covered later on, such as Publish and Subscribe. These offer much more convenience and flexibility than simple cutting, copying, and pasting, although they're slightly more difficult to master.

Cutting, Copying, and Pasting

From your Mac's desktop, first load the application that has the information you'd like to copy into *Word*—for instance, a spreadsheet from *Excel*. Then select or highlight that information, and choose Copy from the application's File menu. By doing this, you're putting a copy of the selection in your Mac's Clipboard (the Clipboard is a little "container" that temporarily stores information so you can easily move it to another place).

Clipboard		
Company	Current Share	Share in 3 Yrs
Largest competitor	55%	30%
Second largest competitor	25%	20%
Third largest competitor	20%	10%
Trey Film Watch	0%	40%

Word lets you see the current contents of the Mac's Clipboard—choose Show Clipboard from the Window menu. In this case, the Clipboard is storing an Excel table.

If your Mac is using MultiFinder in System 6, or Apple's new System 7 operating system, then return to the Mac's desktop and start *Microsoft Word*. In MultiFinder, do this by clicking the application icon to the right of the Mac's menu bar until you've returned to the desktop. Or, if you're running System 7, click the application icon and select the Finder from the application menu (if *Word* is already running in memory, then use these steps to go directly to *Word*). Once in *Word*, position the text cursor at the desired spot in your document, and then choose Paste from the Edit menu. The item you selected in the previous application should appear in your document.

If you're not using MultiFinder or System 7, or if you don't have enough memory to run *Word* and another application at once, then Copy the information in one application, then quit that application, load *Word*, and finally Paste the information into your document.

Using the Mac's Scrapbook. You might also want to use your Mac's Scrapbook as a sort of middleman in the copying and pasting you do between programs. When you copy information to the Clipboard, you're only temporarily storing it. That's because the Clipboard only

Remember that the Mac's Clipboard only holds one piece of information at a time. Don't copy another selection into it until you've pasted your previous selection.

Chapter Nine ▾ Sharing Information

You can cut, copy, and paste text and graphics to and from the Mac's Scrapbook (under the Apple menu). Here I've stored an important graphic for my next business presentation.

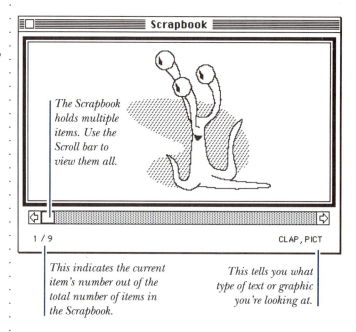

The Scrapbook holds multiple items. Use the Scroll bar to view them all.

This indicates the current item's number out of the total number of items in the Scrapbook.

This tells you what type of text or graphic you're looking at.

holds one piece of copied information at a time—occasionally, you might copy other information in to the Clipboard, and replace the original information you meant to paste into *Word*. The Clipboard also gets erased whenever you turn your Mac off.

But the Mac's Scrapbook stores copied information permanently on disk, so it's always available. To use it, first use the Mac's Copy command to copy any information you'd like. Then choose Scrapbook from the Apple menu (the first menu on the menu bar) to open the Scrapbook. Choose Paste from the Edit menu to commit the information to the Scrapbook. Now you can open whatever *Word* document you'd like and position the text cursor in the appropriate spot. Call up the Scrapbook again and use the scroll bar to locate the information you pasted in before. Select Copy from the Edit menu, and then return back to your *Word* document, and choose Paste from the Edit menu.

Publishing and Subscribing

Use *Word's* Publish and Subscribe feature to share and automatically update information you've incorporated from other programs. You can also use the feature in reverse—to incorporate *Word* documents, or selected parts, into other *Word* documents, or other applications altogether. You can even share data with different Macintoshes on a network. Remember, however, that to take advantage of this, your applications must be written to support System 7, and your Mac must have it installed.

How it works. Publish and Subscribe works like this: select any information you'd like to share in your *Word* document, or that you'd like your *Word* document to share in another application. This selection becomes a "Publisher," since it's the information source. Your Mac automatically copies the contents of that publisher into a new file, called an "Edition," and it's this edition that other computers and applications can incorporate—that is, can "subscribe to." Once this link is established, you can change the original publisher, and the Mac updates its corresponding edition, which in turn gets updated in all of the documents and computers that subscribe to the edition.

Note: Publishers, Editions, Subscribers—this terminology is bewildering at first, but don't despair! It won't be long 'till it's all second nature.

Creating a Publisher in Word

Follow these steps when you want to publish a part of your *Word* document for other applications and documents to subscribe to. If you'd like your document to subscribe to an edition from another application, see *Subscribing to Editions* below.

To publish information in *Word*—that is, to create an edition file—first select the part of your document to publish (this can include graphics) or highlight the entire document. Now choose Create Publisher from the Edit menu, and *Word* presents a File Save box. Select the disk or folder you'd like to hold your edition, and type in a name for the edition. Click the Publish button and

> 💡 *While most of Word's information sharing talents require Apple's System 7, you can use a more limited QuickSwitch feature with the older System 6. See page 199.*

Select text and graphics in your document, and then choose Create Publisher from Word's Edit menu to name the selection's corresponding edition.

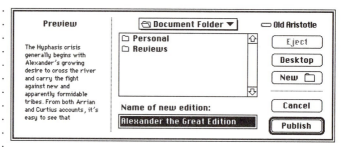

Word copies the information from your publisher into the edition file. With this approach, you can create as many publishers and corresponding editions as you like—even from different parts of the same document.

By the way, *Word* indicates published items in your document by enclosing them in thick gray brackets. You'll need to have *Word's* Show ¶ feature (under the View menu) turned on, however, to see them.

Updating and Canceling a Publisher

Ordinarily, when you make a change to a published part of your document, *Word* updates its corresponding edition as soon as you save the file—this is fine for most of us. You can, however, set *Word* to update editions as soon as they're edited—no saving required, but this option slows *Word* down a bit—or only when you manually tell it to. To do this, place your cursor in a published selection, and then choose Publisher Options from the Edit menu. Select the option you prefer, and click OK.

Updating manually. When you want to update a publisher's edition manually, select the publisher, choose Publisher Options from the Edit menu, and click the Send Edition Now button.

Highlight a published item, choose Publisher Options, and tell Word when to update the item's corresponding edition, or cancel the published item altogether.

Canceling a publisher. To cancel a publisher so it no longer updates its editions, place your text cursor anywhere in the publisher selection. Choose Publisher Options from the Edit menu, and click the Cancel Publisher button. If you want to delete a published selection altogether, cancel the publisher first, and then delete the selection.

Subscribing to Editions

Incorporating an edition—either from another *Word* document, or a different program altogether—means subscribing to it. Place your text cursor at the point where you want to insert the edition, be it text from another *Word* document, or perhaps a graphic from some other application. Choose Subscribe To from the Edit menu, select the appropriate edition from the list of files, and then click the Subscribe button. *Word* responds by copying that edition into your document. If you have the Show ¶ option turned on (under the View menu), you'll see the edition enclosed in thick gray brackets.

Word uses thick, gray brackets to enclose both published items and editions in your documents. To see the brackets, select Show ¶ from the View menu, or click the ¶ icon on Word's Ribbon bar.

Choose Subscribe To from the Edit menu to select and insert an edition in your document. Notice that Word gives a preview of the selected edition.

This gray box indicates the file is an edition.

Updating and Canceling a Subscriber

Ordinarily, *Word* updates a subscribed selection automatically, as soon as an updated edition is available. You can, however, choose to update subscribers manually—select the subscriber, choose Subscriber Options from the Edit menu, and check the Manually option. From now on, *Word* updates only when you tell it to. To do this, select the subscriber, choose Publisher Options from Edit, and click the Get Edition Now button.

Here's a big advantage to using the manual approach when subscribing to text selections from other *Word* documents, or perhaps spreadsheet data. *Word* ordinarily

Highlight an edition in your document, and choose Subscriber Options from the Edit menu to tell Word when to reflect changes to the edition.

Latest Edition tells when the edition was last updated by its publisher. Last Received tells when your document last updated the edition.

doesn't let you edit the text you're subscribing to, and only makes formatting changes—font, size, style—to the entire selection, but not separate words, lines, or paragraphs. With the manual option, however, you can edit text and make formatting changes as you're used to.

Canceling a subscriber. To cancel a subscriber so it's no longer updated by its edition, first select the subscriber in your document—the graphic, imported spreadsheet cells, what have you. Then choose Subscriber Options from the Edit menu, and click the Cancel Publisher button. If you want to remove a subscriber selection from the document altogether, first cancel the subscriber, and then delete the item.

Editing a Subscriber

By choosing the manual subscriber update option in the Subscriber Options box, *Word* lets you edit and format a block of text that you've subscribed to. Unfortunately, every time a subscriber is updated by its edition, it loses the changes you've given it. Therefore, it's a good idea to *not* alter subscriber selections in your document.

If you really want to change some aspect of subscribed information, it's better to change the information from the source—that is, the publisher. Select the desired subscriber in your document, choose Subscriber Options from the Edit menu, and then click the Open Publisher button. *Word* opens the publisher document, and you're free to make your changes to the original source of the subscribed data. The changes are reflected next time you update the corresponding subscriber in your document.

LINKING DOCUMENTS AND OTHER APPLICATIONS

Word's Linking feature works similarly to Publish and Subscribe, except that it links two applications or *Word* documents directly to each other, rather than through a middle-man edition file. Specifically, you copy data from one application or *Word* document, and then paste it into your own document. When that source information is changed, *Word* can automatically update the pasted information. Doing this, however, requires System 7, and enough memory to run two applications simultaneously.

Drawbacks to linking. Unfortunately, Linking isn't as widely supported by other programs as Publish and Subscribe is—that's because it's based on a technology that Microsoft developed alone, and that other programs have not yet adopted (and may never—who knows?). As I write this, Linking only works with *Excel* 3.0 and the mathematical equation editor that's included with *Word*. Nonetheless, we'll quickly run through the feature. Perhaps it will be more widespread in the future.

Creating a Link

First, open the application that you'd like to copy information from. Select the desired information—for instance, a few rows of spreadsheet data in *Excel*—and choose Copy from the Edit menu. Switch back to *Word*, and place your text cursor wherever the copied information should appear. Hold down the Shift key and choose Paste Link from the Edit menu (hold down Shift *before* pulling down the menu)—after a few moments, *Word* pastes the copied information into your document, and surrounds it with thick gray brackets (if you've selected Show ¶ from the Edit menu).

Updating and Canceling Links

By default, *Word* updates your link automatically, as soon as its source is changed. You can, however, set *Word* to update links only when you say so. Besides simply giving you the freedom to choose when an update occurs, this manual approach offers another benefit. With the

Through the Link Options dialog box, you can decide how to update a linked item when there's a change at its source.

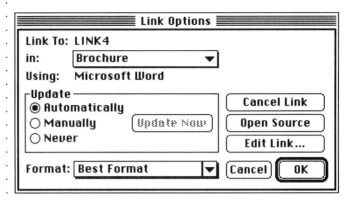

automatic update method, *Word* doesn't let you edit linked text in your documents, and only makes formatting changes—font, size, style—to the entire selection rather than parts of your choosing. With the manual option, however, you can edit text and make formatting changes as you're used to.

To set *Word* for manual link updates, select the linked information in your document, choose Link Options from the Edit menu, and check the Manually option under Update. Likewise, to actually update a link, you'd select the linked item, choose Link Options from Edit, and click the Update Now button.

And if you only want to temporarily disable a link—perhaps you'll want to receive updates later, but just not at that moment—then choose the Never options in the Link Options box.

Canceling a link. When you no longer want information in your document linked to its source, select the linked item and choose Link Options from the Edit menu. Click the Cancel Link button to destroy the link.

Editing Linked Items

You can edit and format linked text in your documents, but your changes will be lost as soon as that information is updated from its linked source again. That's why it's better to change linked information at the source. To do this, first select the link you'd like to alter. Choose Link Options from the Edit menu, and then click the Open Source button. *Word* opens the source document—for instance, an *Excel* spreadsheet—where you can make all your desired adjustments. Save the source document and *Word* will reflect those changes according to the Update option you've set (Automatic, Manually, or Never).

Embedding Information

Word's Embedding feature offers yet another approach to incorporating data from other programs into your documents. The approach is similar to Linking, in that you copy information from the source program, and paste it into *Word*. The difference is that embedding doesn't incorporate merely a *copy* of that source information. Instead, it embeds the actual source into your document, where it's easy to edit and update. Double-click the embedded object—for instance, an *Excel* pie chart—and *Word* opens an object window with all of the related *Excel* commands available (provided *Excel* is also on your hard disk). The advantage is that you don't have to change information from its source anymore—for instance, return to *Excel* everytime the pie chart data should be updated. Instead, you can do the job directly from *Word*. Doing this, however, requires System 7, and enough memory to run two applications simultaneously.

Drawbacks. The drawback is that embedding does not automatically update information from its source, as does Publish and Subscribe, and Linking—if someone changes the *Excel* pie chart from within *Excel*, you won't see that reflected by the embedded chart in your document. Like the Linking feature, too, Embedding uses a technology that Microsoft developed alone, and that hasn't caught on with other programs yet. Consequently, the feature currently works with *Excel* and the mathematical equation editor that's included with *Word*. Chances are, this won't become a mainstream feature, but it's worth quickly covering anyway.

Embedding an Object

First, open the application that has the information you'd like to embed. Select the information—an *Excel* graphic maybe—and choose Copy from the Edit menu. Switch back to *Word*, and place your text cursor wherever you'd like to embed the information. Hold down the Shift key and choose Paste Object from the Edit menu—*Word* embeds the information into your document, and surrounds it with thick gray brackets (you'll see the brackets if you've selected Show ¶ from the Edit menu).

Creating new objects. You can embed an empty object, and then fill it with data. Position your text cursor in the appropriate spot and choose Object from the Insert menu. *Word* asks you what type of object you'd like to create—an *Excel* worksheet or chart are possible two choices. Make the selection, and *Word* creates a new object and opens its object window to the application you specified—*Excel* probably. Use any of the application's commands to build your object, and then choose Close from the File menu to return back to *Word*. The advantage here is that you don't have to separately open the source application (*Excel*) to create the item you'd like to embed. You can do it all from *Word*.

Canceling embedding. Embedding an object can boost the file size of your *Word* documents, since they're storing all the data that makes up the embedded items. To cancel embedding, select the appropriate object, choose Object Options from the Edit menu, and click the Change To Picture button.

Editing an Embedded Object

To edit an object you've embedded in your document, just give it a double-click. *Word* opens its object window, and gives you access to the application that created the object. When you're finished editing, choose Close from the application's File menu to return back to *Word*.

LINKING DATA WITH SYSTEM 6

If your Mac is still using System 6, you're not completely ignored when it comes to linking data with other programs. Using *Word's* QuickSwitch feature, you can copy information from one application—a graphic or chart or spreadsheet data—into your documents. When you make a change to these copied elements in their source applications, you can tell *Word* to reflect those changes in your document.

By the way, this feature only works with a handful of applications, most notably *Microsoft Excel*, and early versions of *SuperPaint*, *MacPaint*, and *MacDraw*. You also need to run Apple's System 6 in MultiFinder mode.

Creating a QuickSwitch Link

Open the application that you'd like to copy information from, select the desired information—for instance, a bar chart in *Excel*—and choose Copy from the Edit menu. Now switch to *Word*, and place your text cursor at the spot where the copied information should appear. Then hold down the Shift key and choose Paste Link from the Edit menu—*Word* pastes the copied information into your document, and surrounds it with thick gray brackets (you'll see the brackets if you've selected Show ¶ from the Edit menu).

Updating and Canceling a Link

To update a link (when you know the source information has been changed in its own application), first select the linked information in your document. Choose Link Options from the Edit menu, and click the Update Now button. And to cancel a link, select the linked informa-

> ❗ *If you're bothering to use System 6's QuickSwitch feature, you'd really be better off by upgrading your Mac to System 7 and recruiting its more advanced information sharing talents. Besides, System 7 is relatively bug-free, and most mainstream software is compatible.*

tion in your document, choose Link Options and click the Cancel Link button.

Editing Linked Information

You can edit and format any linked text in *Word*—for instance, some cells from an *Excel* spreadsheet—but if you update that linked information again, it will lose any changes you've made previously. Therefore, it's better to edit or format linked information from the source. To do this, first select the information you'd like to change in your document. Choose Link Options from the Edit menu, and then click the Open Source button. *Word* opens the source document—for instance, that *Excel* spreadsheet—where you can make all the necessary adjustments. When you're done, hit Command-Comma(,), to switch back to your *Word* document and update the linked information.

OPENING AND SAVING IN OTHER FILE FORMATS

Word lets you open documents created by a great variety of other applications. Not only does it retain their text content, but it also recognizes special formatting such as font specifications, styles (bold, italic, etc.), margins, page breaks—sometimes even embedded graphics and multiple columns. *Word* can also save its own documents in the formats of other programs, so you can transport your work into a wide range of environments—for instance, bring a Mac document over to *WordPerfect* on the IBM PC.

Here are the text file formats that *Word* recognizes:

- ▼ Microsoft Word for the Mac, versions 1.0–4.0
- ▼ Microsoft Word for DOS, versions 1.0–5.5
- ▼ Microsoft Word for Windows, versions 1.0–2.0
- ▼ Microsoft Works for the Mac, version 2.0
- ▼ MacWrite, versions 4.5–5.0
- ▼ MacWrite II

- WordPerfect for the Mac, version 2.0
- WordPerfect for DOS, versions 4.1–5.1
- Interchange Format (RTF)
- Text (Text Only, Text Only With Line Breaks, Text With Layout)
- Stationery

On the graphics side, *Word* also accepts *MacPaint*, PICT, Encapsulated PostScript and TIFF file formats (see page 109 for more information on incorporating these).

Some of *Word's* compatible formats may require explanation. Here goes:

Interchange Format (RTF). Also called Rich Text Format, the Interchange Format is becoming a universal format that many applications recognize. Interchange is useful because it records much of the formatting in your documents, and it's sometimes the only format that *Word* and another application will have in common.

Text. *Word's* Text format comes in three flavors. *Text Only* saves your documents without formatting (such as font, point size, style, margins, indents, line spacing, section breaks, and page breaks). Use this only if a particular application won't accept your document in another format. Saving in *Text Only With Line Breaks* also doesn't record your formatting, but it *does* mark the end of each line of a document with a paragraph return. This is handy when you want to keep lines at certain lengths, perhaps for sending text to an electronic mail system like CompuServe or MCI Mail. *Text With Layout* foregos most character formatting, but line and paragraph spacing, tabs, indents, and tables are substituted with spaces, to preserve the document's layout look.

Stationery. This isn't a file format to interchange with other programs. It simply lets you to save documents as templates, which you can repeatedly apply to documents with similar layouts and formats. For instance, you might save a standard invoice form as a stationery template, and call it up whenever you're writing invoices.

> *If you're preparing text to send to an electronic mail system, you'll probably want to save it in the Text Only With Line Breaks format.*

CHAPTER NINE ▾ Sharing Information

Opening and Saving Other File Formats

To open a document in a different file format, choose Open from the File menu. Make sure the List Files of Type button is at a setting that will show your format type. For instance, if the button reads *Word* Files, you won't see graphics, or WordPerfect documents listed in the file selector. Choose an option like All Files, All Readable Files, or a particular file format if necessary (if you still can't find your file, perhaps it's not in a format that *Word* recognizes). When you find the file, select it and click the Open button.

💡 *Before you save a document in a different format, be sure to save a copy in Word's Normal format. It's a precaution, so you'll always have the original document and formatting to return to if the need arises.*

Saving in other formats. To save a *Word* document in a different file format, use the same approach. Choose Save As from the File menu, type in the file's name, and then pick the appropriate format from the Save File as Type button—for instance, choose the *MacWrite*, or *Word for Windows* format.

Unrecognized formats. If *Word* doesn't seem to open or save a format that I've listed here, then you may not have the appropriate converter file installed (*Word* uses special "converter files" to make it compatible with some formats—these are supposed to be kept in the Word Command folder in your main *Word* folder). To fix this problem, quit *Word*, and find the appropriate converter file in your *Word* folder or the original program disks from Microsoft. Place the file into *Word's* Command folder. Then try to open or save in the desired format again.

```
Save File as Type
Normal                              ▼
  ✓Normal
  Text Only
  Text Only with Line Breaks
  Microsoft Mac Word 3.x
  Interchange Format (RTF)
  Stationery
  MacWrite
  MacWrite II 1.x
  Text with Layout
  Word for DOS
  Word for Windows 1
  ▼
```

In the Save As dialog box, click the Save File as Type button to choose the appropriate document format.

These are some of the file converters that allow Word to save your documents in other program formats. Make sure that they're in Word's Commands folder to work properly.

PLACING WORD DOCUMENTS IN OTHER PROGRAMS

You may be preparing documents in *Word* that are destined to go into other software—for instance, you might write a newsletter story that will be laid out in PageMaker, *XPress* or another page layout program. Since *Word* is such a popular and pervasive program, you can expect any other Mac software to recognize *Word's* document format. That doesn't just mean reading *Word's* text, but also much of its formatting, such as font, size, style, line spacing, tabs, indents, margins, style sheets, and so on.

What doesn't work. Other formatting, however, won't work outside of *Word*, and may cause problems when you try to bring your documents into other programs. For instance, W*ord's* special tables, positioned text and graphics, multiple columns, sections divisions, footnotes, and headers and footers won't transfer to most applications. You'll probably have to recreate these elements in the destination program.

CHAPTER 10

Customizing Word

What's Inside

- ▼ Word's Default Preferences
- ▼ Customizing Word's Menus
- ▼ Making Keyboard Shortcuts
- ▼ Saving Your Customizations

One of *Word's* most appreciable aspects is that you can customize it to suit your own preferences, from simple things like setting a measurement system for the Ruler to completely overhauling menus and keyboard shortcuts. It's a fantastic feature that no other Mac word processor quite matches.

WORD'S DEFAULT PREFERENCES

Many of *Word's* features follow default settings—for instance, the program uses inches as its standard measuring unit, it sets type in Geneva at 12 points, and there are dozens of other settings that tell it how to behave. Fortunately, you can change all of these to suit your own style. You might have *Word* make automatic backup copies of all your documents, or perhaps open the spelling checker with foreign dictionaries.

Setting Preferences

Choose Preferences under the Tools menu to call up the appropriate dialog box. Notice the column of icons on the box's left side—these icons divide *Word's* preferences into related categories, such as General, or View, or Spelling. The Preferences box opens with the General category, but you can scroll through and click any icon to see its related settings. Specify your preferences by checking and unchecking various options and entering values. Then you can click another category icon, or leave Preferences by clicking the window's close box. *Word* follows your custom settings from that point on.

> *Your preferences are saved in the settings file that is currently opened in Word (usually the file, Word Settings (5)). You can create multiple settings files that each hold different preferences. See the section, Saving Your Customizations below.*

Preferences Available

General. *Your Name* is the name *Word* will use in its Document Summary feature (see page 36), while *Your Initials* are used to stamp any voice annotations you make in a document (page 153). *Custom Paper Size* sets a custom paper size for your documents, as opposed to standard Letter or Legal sizes *Word* supports. Use *Measurement Unit* to specify whether *Word* should use values in inches, centimeters, and so on. *Smart Quotes* automatically inserts true, typeset-quality quotation marks ("like

The General category in the Preferences box. Keeping Smart Quotes and Background Repagination are especially recommended.

these") for straight quotes ("like these") as you type—I recommend turning this option on. *Background Repagination* means that *Word* automatically updates page numbers, page breaks, and other elements as you type and format your document. This is handy, but it may slow *Word* down in long documents. In that case, you might turn it off and manually repaginate with the Repaginate Now command under Tools. *Include Formatted Text in Clipboard* means that the text you cut, copy, and paste retains various formatting, such as bold or italic type, or centered paragraph alignment. Finally, *Drag-and-Drop Text Editing* refers to the ability to select text, and then drag it anywhere in your document (no cutting or pasting required—see page 25).

View. The options under *Show* define which elements *Word* displays on-screen when you open a document. *Hidden Text* refers to the character style—see page 55 for details. *Table Gridlines* are the dotted lines between rows and columns of a table—these don't print, but help you organize your tables. *Text Boundaries in Page Layout View* displays dotted rectangles around text areas, headers, footers, and framed text in *Word's* Page Layout view—this sometimes helps identify a page's various elements. Checking *Picture Placeholders* tells *Word* to display all graphics as gray rectangles—the graphics will still print fine, but displaying them in this way helps *Word* work a little faster.

CHAPTER TEN ▼ Customizing Word

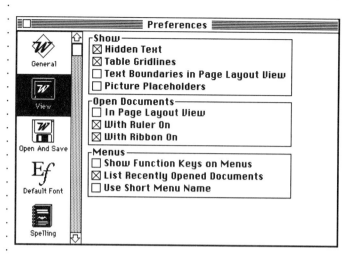

The View icon in the Preferences box lets you decide which elements will appear on-screen in your documents.

The *Open Documents* options are obvious—choose these so *Word* automatically opens documents in the Page Layout, rather than Normal view, and turns on its Ruler and Ribbon.

Under *Menus, Show Function Keys on Menus* tells *Word* to display the equivalent keyboard commands next to their respective menu items. It helps to learn these handy shortcuts. And *List Recently Opened Documents* tells *Word* to list under the File menu the last four documents you've opened—this way they're quickly accessible without using the file selector.

- **Open and Save.** *Always Interpret RTF* means *Word* always translates Rich Text Format documents (also called Interchange Format, which is designed so you can open formatted documents created in other programs) without asking you first. *Always Make Backup* means *Word* will save a second copy of your documents, under the name "Backup of *document name*." It's handy if you're into meticulous backups, but not requisite. With *Allow Fast Saves, Word* saves your documents quicker when you use the Save command, but they grow in size with each save. This option is recommended, but to fight the size problem, just use the Save As command every once in a while. Save As brings the document to its smallest size. *Prompt For Summary Info* means that *Word* always asks you for author, subject, and comments information when

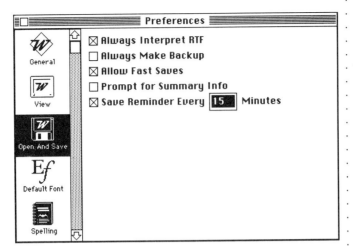

The Open and Save category in Word's Preferences box.

you save a new document (see page 36 for details). And with *Save Reminder Every ( ) Minutes, Word* reminds you to save documents at the time interval you specify.

Default Font. *Default Font* and *Size* let you set the font that *Word* automatically uses in new documents. Your choice will be inserted into the Normal Style of *Word's* style sheet (see page 61 for more about Styles).

Spelling and Grammar. *Word's* spelling and grammar checker both have many preferences, but you can set them directly through the Spelling and Grammar windows by clicking the windows' Options button. I explain the preferences in their respective sections—spelling on page 84, and grammar on page 87.

Thesaurus and Hyphenation. These preferences let you set the default language dictionary used by *Word's* thesaurus and hyphenation feature, in theory. In practice, *Word* only comes with English language dictionaries, so there really are no options, unless you have other add-on dictionaries from another software company.

CHAPTER TEN ▾ Customizing Word

CUSTOMIZING MENUS AND KEYBOARD COMMANDS

Word lets you redesign its interface by adding and removing menu items, and defining your own keyboard shortcuts. For instance, if you often use the Word Count feature, you can assign the function its own keyboard command. Or if you never use the Index or Table of Contents commands, you can remove them from *Word's* menus. To do these and similar feats, you'll choose Commands from the Tools menu.

The Tools menu before and after being customized. Notice how I've removed some commands from the customized menu, while adding keyboard shortcuts for other commands.

Tools	
Spelling...	⌘L
Grammar...	⌘⇧G
Thesaurus...	
Hyphenation...	
Word Count...	
Renumber...	
Sort	
Calculate	⌘=
Repaginate Now	
Preferences...	
Commands...	⌘⇧⌥C

Tools	
Spelling...	⌘L
Grammar...	⌘⇧G
Thesaurus...	⌘⇧T
Hyphenation...	⌘⇧H
Word Count...	⌘⇧W
Repaginate Now	
Preferences...	
Commands...	⌘⇧⌥C

Customizing Menus

Besides general menu items, you can also add and remove dialog box options, commands on buttons in dialog boxes, and functions that are ordinarily activated by clicking icons on *Word's* Ruler and Ribbon. If you're adding these commands, you can also specify which menu they'll appear under. Choose Commands from the Tools menu to bring up the appropriate dialog box.

Adding functions. Select the function to add from the Commands scroll box, which lists every feature of the software alphabetically. In the Menu box, the top button displays the preferred menu for this feature to appear under. Click it to choose any other menu. Click the Add Below button to choose where on a menu the new feature appears—at the top, bottom, or under an

Customizing Word ▾ CHAPTER TEN

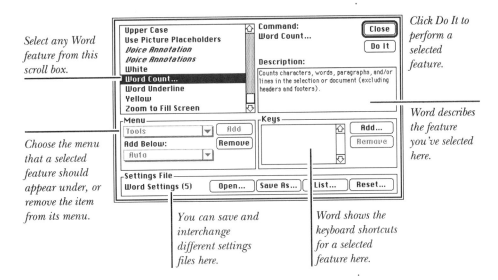

existing menu item. Now click the Add button (if the function is already on the menu, or can't be added, this button will be gray).

Removing functions. Select the feature from the Commands scroll box, and then click the Remove button. Any item you remove, by the way, still remains in the Commands list, so it can easily be added again.

Quickly Adding and Removing Menu Items

There's a quicker way to add and remove menu items, without calling up the Commands box. It's handy because you don't have to search through a long feature list. The minor drawback is that this alternative doesn't let you choose which menu an added feature appears under—*Word* decides instead.

To quickly add a function to a menu, call up the dialog box, Ruler, Ribbon, or other item you'd like to add. For instance, if you're adding Smart Quotes to the menu, call up the Preferences dialog box first. Press Command-Option-Plus (the plus sign on the *keyboard*, not the numeric keypad) and *Word's* mouse pointer becomes a large plus sign. Now click the item to add—a check box, a selection under a drop-down button, etc. *Word* adds the feature to your menus.

❗ *Occasionally, you might want to access a command not on the menus, but without installing it on a menu. Open the Commands box, select a feature and then click the Do It button. Word will activate this feature, as if you've selected it from a menu.*

211

CHAPTER TEN ▾ Customizing Word

To quickly remove a menu item, press Command-Option-Minus (the minus sign on the *keyboard*, not the numeric keypad), and the mouse pointer turns into a large minus sign. Now pull down a menu and choose the item to remove.

By the way, if you call up either the plus or minus sign command, and then decide you don't want to add or remove a menu item, just hit Escape.

Creating a New Menu

You can create an entirely new menu, called the Work menu, to list individual documents, glossary files and entries, and style sheet styles that you use regularly. Listing them on a separate menu makes accessing them convenient. For instance, if you often use a standard letter form, you might place that document file on the Work menu so you can choose it without browsing through the file selector.

Word displays the Work menu on the far right side of the menu bar—but only after you've added an item to it. To add an item, first open the dialog box or file selector box that contains it. Press Command-Option-Plus (on the *keyboard*, not the numeric keypad) to see the large plus sign pointer, and then select the item, Style name or document file. To remove, press Command-Option-Minus and select the item under the Work menu.

Customizing Keyboard Shortcuts

Select Commands from the Tools menu to call up the appropriate dialog box. Select a function from the Commands scroll box, and *Word* displays its associated keyboard shortcuts in the Keys box.

Adding shortcuts. Click the Add button in the Keys box, and *Word* asks you to type in a key combination. Press the keys combination you'd like to add—your keyboard shortcut needs to include either the Command or Control key (Shift and Option are optional), plus a regular character from the keyboard—for instance, Command-S, or Control-Shift-L. If you're making a combination with a character from the numeric keypad, you can use Shift and Option alone, such as Option-1, or

---

Work
Project Notes
Thank You Letter

Body text
Caption
Table Style

I've created this Work menu to quickly access Word documents, and style sheet styles that I use regularly.

❗ *If you're not sure if a key combination is already in use, choose Commands from the Tools menu, and then type in the combination. Word either selects the command that owns the shortcut, or does nothing to indicate the shortcut doesn't exist.*

Shift-*. If your key combination is acceptable to *Word*, it's added to the Keys box. If the combination exists already for another command, *Word* asks if you want to remove the combination from the conflicting command.

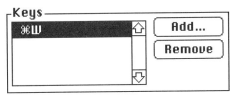

Select an item from the Commands scroll box, and then you can add or remove a corresponding keyboard shortcut.

Removing shortcuts. Highlight the shortcut in the Keys box, and click the Remove button.

Quickly Adding Keyboard Shortcuts

There's a quicker way to add keyboard shortcuts without calling up the Commands box. Call up the dialog box, Ruler, Ribbon, or other item you'd like to create the shortcut for. For instance, if you're adding Merge Cells to the menu, call up the Table Layout dialog box first. Press Command-Option-Plus (the plus sign on the *numeric keypad*, not the keyboard) and *Word's* mouse pointer becomes a large command sign. Now select the item to add—a check box, a selection under a drop-down button, etc. *Word* asks you to type your keyboard shortcut, and then adds it to the system.

Word changes your mouse pointer into a command sign to indicate it's ready to add a keyboard shortcut.

To remove a shortcut, you'll have to use the Commands feature. See the section above.

SAVING YOUR CUSTOMIZATIONS

Whenever you make changes through the Preferences command, or customize menus or keyboard shortcuts, or set other defaults, *Word* automatically saves your changes in a special file called *Word Settings (5)* (which sits in your Mac's System Folder, or the System Folder's Preferences folder for System 7). This file describes to *Word* exactly how menus are arranged, which keyboard commands are active, which options are set, and so on. It's a blueprint to *Word's* entire interface.

❗ *To see or print a list of all of Word's commands, or just its current menus and keyboard shortcuts, choose Command from the Tools menu, and then click List from the Settings File box.*

Fortunately, you can create multiple settings files—each with distinct interfaces—and install them according to the occasion. For instance, if a number of people at your office use the same copy of *Word*, each could use his own settings file with the custom set-up they're most comfortable with. Or you could create a number of files oriented specifically to a certain task—for instance, an all-purpose file, and then a version specifically geared for making tables, where all of *Word's* table functions are listed on the menus.

```
┌Settings File─────────────────────────────────────┐
│ Helmut's Settings    [ Open... ][ Save As... ][ List... ][ Reset... ] │
```

The Settings File box in the Commands dialog box lets you interchange custom settings files within Word. You can create a settings file for yourself, and perhaps another file for an officemate or family member.

- **Creating a settings file.** Finish your customization, and then choose Commands from the Tools menu. Click the Save As button in the Settings File box. Type in the name for your new file—say, *Leigh's Word Settings*—and save.

- **Opening a settings file.** To load in a new settings file, open the Command box, and click Open in the Settings File box. Choose the file, and *Word* loads it and customizes its interface according to the file's specifications.

- **Restoring Word's original settings.** To go back to *Word's* original settings, first make sure you've loaded in the Word Settings (5) file. Then click the Reset button in the Settings File box.

Keyboard Shortcuts

Keyboard shortcuts (aka keyboard commands) are convenient alternatives to calling up features and choosing menu items and dialog box options with the mouse. Suppose, for instance, that you're typing away, and want to get a word count of your text. Instead of taking your hand off the keys, moving the mouse to the appropriate menu, selecting the Word Count feature, etc., you can simply hold down the Command key, and press W—the Word Count box pops right up. Admittedly, this doesn't sound like some revolutionary feature, but trust me, once you become comfortable with *Word* and word processing in general, you'll appreciate keyboard shortcuts to no end. They're a power user's delight.

By the way, some shortcuts are only available if you have Apple's extended keyboard, or some third-party equivalent. I've noted these shortcuts with "ext. kb" in parenthesis. Other shortcuts use numbers from your keyboard's numeric keypad (which is laid out like a calculator). I note these with "numeric kp."

Shortcuts to Menu Items

Here's a listing of keyboard shortcuts to many of Word's menu items. If Word doesn't provide a shortcut to a particular feature you use often, remember that you can create your own shortcuts (see page 210).

File Menu

New	Command-N
Open	Command-O
Close	Command-W
Save	Command-S
Save As	Shift-F7 (ext. kb)
Print Preview	Command-Option-I
Page Setup	Shift-F8 (ext. kb)
Print	Command-P
Quit	Command-Q

Edit Menu

Undo	Command-Z
Repeat	Command-Y
Cut	Command-X
Copy	Command-C
Paste	Command-V
Paste Object	Command-F4 (ext. kb)
Page Link	Option-F4 (ext. kb)
Select All	Command-A
Find	Command-F
Replace	Command-H
Go To	Command-G
Glossary	Command-K
Insert Glossary Entry	Command-Backspace (type in entry name)

View Menu

Normal View	Command-Option-N
Page Layout View	Command-Option-P
Outline View	Command-Option-O
Ribbon	Command-Option-R
Ruler	Command-R
Show/Hide ¶	Command-J
Footnotes	Command-Option-Shift-S

Insert Menu

Page Break	Shift-Enter
Section Break	Command-Enter
Footnote	Command-E

Format Menu

Character	Command-D
Paragraph	Command-M
Section	Option-F14 (ext. kb)
Document	Command-F14 (ext.kb)
Style	Command-T

Keyboard Shortcuts

Revert to Style	Command-Shift-Space
Plain Text	Command-Shift-Z
Bold	Command-B
Italic	Command-I
Underline	Command-U

Font Menu

Font Size Up	Command-]
Font Size Down	Command-[

Tools Menu

Spelling	Command-L
Grammar	Command-Shift-G
Hyphenation	Shift-F15 (ext. kb)
Word Count	Option-F15 (ext. kb)
Renumber	Command-F15 (ext. kb)
Calculate	Command-Equal (=)
Commands	Command-Option-Shift-C

Window Menu

Help	Command-/
New Window	Shift-F5 (ext. kb)

Formatting Text

Bold	Command-B
Italic	Command-I
Underline	Command-U
Word Underline	Command-Shift-]
Dbl Underline	Command-Shift-[
Dot Underline	Command-Shift-\
Strikethru	Command-Shift-/
Outline	Command-Shift-D
Shadow	Command-Shift-W
Small Capitals	Command-Shift-H
All Capitals	Command-Shift-K
Hidden Text	Command-Shift-X
Subscript	Command-Shift-Minus
Superscript	Command-Shift-Plus
Change Font	Command-Shift-E (type in name)
Symbol Font	Command-Shift-Q
Next Larger Size	Command-Shift->
Next Smaller Size	Command-Shift-<
Increase Font 1 pt	Command-]
Decrease Font 1pt	Command-[

Formatting Paragraphs

Normal Paragraph Style	Command-Shift-P
Apply New Style (type style name)	Command-Shift-S
Left-Aligned	Command-Shift-L
Centered	Command-Shift-C
Right-Aligned	Command-Shift-R
Justified	Command-Shift-J
First Line Indent	Command-Shift-F
"Nest" Paragraph	Command-Shift-N
"Unnest"	Command-Shift-M
Hanging Indent	Command-Shift-T
Double Space	Command-Shift-Y
Paragraph Space	Command-Shift-O

Moving Throughout a Document

Up, Down, Left. Right	Corresponding Keyboard Arrows or 8, 2, 4, 6 on numeric keypad
Previous Word	Command-Left Arrow
Next Word	Command-Right Arrow
Next Table Cell	Tab
Previous Cell	Shift-Tab
Beginning of Line	7 (numeric keypad)
End of Line	1 (numeric keypad)
Previous Sentence	Command-7 (numeric kp)
Next Sentence	Command-1 (numeric kp)
Next Page	Command-Page Down (ext. kb)
Previous Page	Command-Page Up (ext. kb)
Top of Paragraph	Command-Up Arrow
Next Paragraph	Command-Down Arrow
Top of Window	Command-5, Home
Bottom of Window	End (ext. kb)
Start of Document	Command-9 (numeric kp)
End of Document	Command-3 (numeric kp)
Scroll Up 1 Screen	9 (numeric kp)
Scroll Down	3 (numeric kp)
Scroll Up 1 Line	* (numeric kp)
Scroll Down	+ (numeric kp)

Selecting Text

You can select text with keyboard shortcuts, either by characters, words, lines, sentences, or the entire document. To choosing all the text in a document, use Command-A, for Select All. To select portions of text, first use the keyboard shortcuts listed in the previous category, *Moving Throughout a Document,* but hold down the Shift key as well. For instance, the command to move *Word's* text cursor to the next word is Command-Right Arrow. Therefore, the command to *select* the next word is Command-Shift-Right Arrow.

Outlining Shortcuts

Outline View	Command-Option-O
Promote Heading	Option-Left Arrow
Demote Heading	Option-Right Arrow
Heading Up	Option-Up Arrow
Heading Down	Option-Down Arrow
Make Body Text	Command-Right Arrow
Expand Heading	Option-Shift-Right Arrow
Collapse Heading	Option-Shift-Right Arrow
Show All Text	Option-Shift-Left Arrow
First Line Text	Option-Shift-Down Arrow
Toggle Formatting	Option-Shift-Up Arrow

Other Keyboard Shortcuts

Getting Help	Command-?
Add Item to Menu	Command-Option-=
Remove Item	Command-Option-Hyphen
Make Key Shortcut	Command-Shift-Option-Left Arrow

Using the above key commands usually changes *Word's* regular I-beam or arrow cursor into a special symbol (an large plus, minus, command or question mark symbol). Use the mouse to then select a menu item or dialog box option to affect (perhaps to remove that item from the menu, create its keyboard command, etc.).

Choosing Menu Items with the Keyboard

You can use the keyboard to choose any item on *Word's* menu—whether it has a corresponding keyboard command or not). First press Command-Tab to activate *Word's* menu bar (it becomes inverted in black). Use the Left and Right Arrow keys to move to any menu you want, and then use the Up and Down Arrow keys to move to a specific item on a particular menu. Hit Return to select the item.

Here's an alternative that I find a little more convenient: instead of using the Up and Down Arrow keys to move to a particular menu item, you can type the first letter of the item's name—for instance, once you've moved to the Format menu, typing "S" selects the Section command. Type the letter again to move to the next item that starts with that letter. For instance, type "S" to select the Section command, and then type "S" again to select Style.

Choosing Dialog Box Options

Instead of opening one of *Word's* dialog boxes (such as the Document or Print box) and then using the mouse to click its various list boxes, check boxes, and radio buttons, you can do this all from the keyboard.

Next Text Box	Tab
Previous Text Box	Shift-Tab
Next Option Box	Command-Tab
Previous Box	Command-Shift-Tab

(When you've moved to an option box, it's indicated by a slowly flashing gray underline)

Select Option Box   Command-Spacebar
(On some occasions, you can also choose an option by pressing Command and then the initial letter of the desired option. For instance, in the Character dialog box, pressing Command-H checks and unchecks the Hidden text style).

Display List Box	Command-Spacebar
Highlight List Items	Up and Down Arrow
Choose List Item	Return, Enter

Window Tricks

Go to Next Window	Command-Option-W
Open/Close Panes	Command-Option-S
Zoom In/Out	Command-Shift-]

Mouse Tricks

You can open certain dialog boxes and feature windows by double-clicking the mouse in areas of a document window.

Paragraph Box	Indent Marker on Ruler
Go To Page Box	Page Number Box (lower-left of window)

Keyboard Shortcuts

Style Sheet Box   Style Name Box
                        (lower-middle of window)
Character Box   Any open area of Ribbon
Section Box   Any Section Marker Line
Document Box   Margin Markers on Ruler
Footnote Window   Any Footnote Reference #
Open/Close   Split Bar of Window
Window Panes
Zoom In/Out   Title Bar of Window
of Window

INDEX

Exclamation marks (!) indicate margin tips.

A

Adding
  items to a menu
    quickly 211–212
Addressing
  envelopes
    when printing 182–183
Adobe Type Manager 54
Aligning
  frames to reference points 151–153
  text and graphics ! 152
Alignment
  of tables 68
  of text
    from the Ruler 49
"All Files" 109
"All Readable Files" 109
"Allow Fast Saves" (Open and Save Preferences) 208–209
Alphabetical headings
  choosing for an Index 128–129
Alphabetizing 157–158
"Always Interpret RTF" (Open and Save Preferences) 208–209
"Always Suggest" (Spelling checker) 84
Annotations, voice 153–155
Antonyms 89
Apply
  in Paragraph Command 57
Apply button 55
  in Character Command 55
"Apply To" (Borders) 113, 114
Applying styles (from Style Sheets) 62
Arc tool 106
Arguments, Index
  using to format 129
Arranging information
  alphabetically and numerically 157–158
Arrowhead tool 108
ASCII 162
Assembling. See Compiling
Attributes
  paragraph
    finding and replacing 95
  text
    finding and replacing 95–96
Auto spacing 56
"Auto-numbered Reference" (Footnote) 132

B

"Background Repagination" 28
"Background Repagination" (Preferences) 207
Backup files
  automatically making 34
Bad grammar. See Grammar checker
"Based On" (Style) 62
"Best" (Printing) 175–176
Binding books
  role of gutters in 75
Black and white
  printing from LaserWriter 175
Bold type style
  choosing through the Ribbon 47
Borders 57, 111–115
  "Apply To" 113, 114
  applying 111–113
    to paragraphs 113
    to tables 113
  basics of 112–113
  box areas for multiple paragraphs and tables
    examples of 114
  customizing 112–113
  dealing with complicated 113–115
  dialog box 112
  "From Text" 113
  how to build into a Style Sheet ! 113
  in tables 69
  removing ! 56
Box character
  as heading symbol in Outlines 139
Boxes. See Borders
Brackets, gray
  to indicate "Published" items 192
    example of 193
"By Example" (Renumber) 60

C

.c. 119–120, 124–125, 127
Codes
  Table of Contents
    in multiple tables 124–125
Calculating 156
  adding
    columns 156
    rows 156
    table numbers 156

219

Canceling
   links 195–196
   "Publisher" 192–193
Captions
   positioning 148
"Catch" (Grammar checker) 87
Cells
   applying borders and lines to 113
   in data documents 161
   table
      dialog box 67
      merging 68
Character Command 53–55
   Apply button 55
   Color 54
   dialog box 54
      gray boxes in 54
   formatting text through
      how to 53
   "Hidden" style in 55
   styles for type in 55
Characters
   attributes of
      finding and replacing 95
   special
      formatting codes for 95
      in Find and Replace 94–95
Chooser 172–173
"Clear" (Find and Replace) 96
Clipboard
   finding out what's in ! 110
   limitations of ! 189
   MultiFinder and 189
   storing calculations in 156
   using to import graphics from other
      programs 109–110
   using to share information with other
      programs 189–191
   using with limited memory 189
   using with System 6 189
   using with System 7 189
   viewing current contents of 189
Codes
   cross-reference 130
   Index 125, 126
      for arguments 129
   Table of Contents 119–120, 127
      for multilevel entries 121
      viewing through Preferences ! 120
Collapsing
   headings in Outlines 141–142
"Collect" (Table of Contents) 121
Color
   in Character Command 54
   printing from a LaserWriter 175

Columns
   adding 156
   applying borders and lines to 113
   icon for 47
   icons for sizing 76
   in tables
      resizing 67
   resizing 76
   setting from Section's Format menu 76
   setting from the Ribbon 76, 48
   setting up 76
   varying in the same document 76–77
Commands
   accessing those not on the menu ! 211
   customizing 210–212
   dialog box for 211
   keyboard
      making your own 42
   restoring *Word* 5.0's original 214
   sharing customized 214
   to see or print a list of *Word* 5.0's ! 213
Commands folder
   Word 5.0's 21
Commas
   "delimited" text 65
Compiling
   Index 128–129
   Table of Contents 121–122
      importance of recompiling ! 122
Computing 156
   math function operators for 156
   totals
      limitations of ! 156
Continuation Notice (Footnotes) 137
Continuation Separator line 136
Controls, keyboard. *See* Keyboard
Converters, file
   examples of 202
Converting
   existing text into tables 65
"Copies" (Printing) 175
Copy
   with graphics 108
Copying
   information from other software pro-
      grams 188–191
   text 25
Copying (pirating) *Word* 5.0 22
"Count By" (Line Numbers) 58
"Cover Page" (Printing) 175
"Create Publisher" 191–192
Cropping graphics 111
Cross 141
   as heading symbol in Outlines 139
Cross-references (Index) 130
   code for 130

Cursor
  text
    moving within a document   27
    positioning   23
Customizing
  dictionaries
    creating   83
  keyboard shortcuts   212–213
  menus
    by adding functions   210–211
    by removing functions   211
    example of   210
  page sizes
    how to set as a default   74
    setting   74
  saving   213–214
  sharing changes made in   214
Cutting   25
  graphics   108
  information from other software programs   188–191
  text   25

D

Data
  entering   161
    from other programs   161–162
DATA command   160, 163
  importance of when merging   165
"Data Document Builder" dialog box   160
Data documents
  adding data from other programs to   161
  adding fields to   161
  creating main documents from   164
  fields in
    adding headers to   162–163
  in Print Merge   159–162
  merging
    with main   164–165
Database
  Word 5.0 as   160–163
"Default Font" (Preferences)   209
Defaults   206–209. *See also* Preferences
  creating your own through style sheets !   63
  setting   206
  setting for printing   177
"Define" (Style)   61
Deleting
  graphics   108
  sections   73
Delimited text
  tab and comma   65
Demoting
  headings in outline to body text   140

Designing
  documents   72–78
"Destination" (printing option from LaserWriter)   175
Dialog boxes
  Borders   112
  Character Command   54
  Chooser   173
  Commands   211
  commands in
    keyboard shortcuts for   41–42
  Data Document Builder   160
  File Series   144, 186
  Find and Replace   93, 96
  Find File   37, 38
  Footnote   132
  for opening existing documents   35
  Frames   151
  Glossary   97
  glossary   98
  Grammar   85
  Grammar Explanation   86
  Header   78
  Help   42
  Hyphenation   91
  Insert Table   65
  keyboard commands for
    !   42
  LaserWriter's Option
    example of   179
  Line Numbers   58
  Link Options   196
  Page Setup
    for the ImageWriter   180
    for the LaserWriter   177
  Paragraph Command   56
  Pictures   109
  Preferences   87, 207
  Print
    for LaserWriter   174
  Print Merge   165
  Renumber (paragraph)   60
  Replace   93, 96
  Section   73
  Spelling checker   82
  Style (sheets)   62
  Subscriber Options   194
  Summary Info   36
  Table Cells   67, 69
  Table Layout   68
  Table of Contents   121
  Tables   65
  Thesaurus   89
  Word Count   92

221

Dictionaries 83–84
   adding words to 84
   custom
      creating 83
      how to work with 83
   editing 84
   existing
      how to open 83
      selecting 83
Distorted imported graphics
   preventing 111
Dividing 156
Document Statistics 87–88
Document windows 39–40
   anatomy of 39
   multiple 40
   splitting 39–40
      undoing a split 40
   title bar in 39
Documents. *See also* Files
   as related to outlines 138
   breaking into multiple parts 72
   data
      creating 160
      creating main documents from 164
      "Data Document Builder" dialog box 160
      in Print Merge 159
   designing 72–78
   entering data into 161
   folder of preformatted
      label files in for printing 166
   linked
      printing 185–186
   linking 144–145, 195–196
      dialog box for 144
   main
      creating from Data Document 163
      creating from existing data document 164
      in Print Merge 159
   merging 164–165
   moving around in 26–27
   multiple
      printing 174
   opening
      existing 34–35
      "Graphic Files" 35
      "List Files of Type" 35
      new 22
      "Readable Files" 35
   recently opened 35
   sample and practice. *See also* Templates
   saving. *See* Saving documents

Documents (continued)
   starting 22–26
   summarizing 36
      turning "Summary Info" on and off 36
   viewing 29–31
   Word 5.0
      placing in other programs 203
Double-arrow
   as heading demoter in Outline 140
Downloadable fonts 179
"Draft" (Printing) 176
"Drag-and-Drop" method of moving text 25
   disabling 25
"Drag-and-Drop Text Editing" (Preferences) 207
Dragging
   frames 149
   text 25
Drawing 104–105
   patterns
      examples of 108
   program in *Word* 5.0 104–107
      limitations of 108
   tools for 104
Driver file, printer 172
   icons for 172
Duplication tool 107

E
"Edit Picture" 109
Editing. *See also* Formatting
   dictionaries 84
   glossaries ! 98
   linked items 196–197
   text 25–26
      linked 200
"Editions" 191
   subscribing to 193
Electronic mail
   sending text through ! 201
Ellipse tool 106
Embedding 197–199
   canceling 198
   drawbacks to 197
   feature in action 198
   objects 197–198
      creating new from empty 198
      editing 199
   with System 7 197
Encapsulated PostScript graphics
   importing 109
ENDIF… 166

Endings
line
not coinciding with what's on the screen 178
Entries
footnote 132–133
Index 126–127
combining with Table of Contents 127–128
not directly in your text 126
Table of Contents
codes for multilevel 121
combining with Index 127–128
creating 119–120
making ones not in the text 120
multilevel 120–121
removing ! 120
Envelopes
feeding into a LaserWriter 183
feeding into an ImageWriter 183
printing 182–183
how to address for 182–183
margins for 183
using Landscape mode for 183
templates for ! 183
EPS files. *See* PostScript files
Equipment
necessary for using *Word* 5.0 20
Excel 110
adding data from 161, 162
Excel 3.0
linking with 195
Expanding
headings in Outlines 141–142
"Explain" (Grammar checker) 86

F

Facing pages
how to set 75
"Fast Save" 34
"Faster" (Printing) 176
"Faster Bitmap Printing" 178
Feeding
envelopes
into a LaserWriter 183
into an ImageWriter 183
Fields, data
adding to tables 161
headers for
adding 162–163
inserting from documents 163–164
names 160
"50% Reduction" (Printing) 180

File converters
examples of 202
File formats
other
opening and saving *Word* 5.0 files as 202
unrecognized 202
Word 5.0's
opening and saving in those other than 200–202
File Series dialog box 144, 186
File settings. *See* Settings file
FileMaker Pro
adding data from 161–162
Files. *See also* Documents
finding. *See* Find File
glossary
merging 99
opening new 99
saving 99
huge
how to avoid 34
multiple
in glossaries 98–99
preformatted
for mailing labels. *See also* Templates
Word 5.0
placing in other programs 203
Fill tools 108
Find and Replace 92–94
character 95
dialog box 93, 96
distinctions between 92–93
how to avoid disasters in ! 94
list of number of changes made through 93
"Match Case" 94
"Match Whole Word" 93
paragraph attributes 95
semi-automatic 93
simple text 93
special characters in 94–95
styles 96
text attributes 95–96
Find File 36–37
dialog box 37, 38
"First Footer" 79
"First Header" 79
Flesch Reading Ease statistics 88
Flesch-Kinkaid statistics 88
"Flip Horizontal" (LaserWriter) 179
Flip tool 107
"Flip Vertical" (LaserWriter) 179
"Font Substitution" (Printing) 177

Fonts. *See also* Style of Type; Character Command
  choosing 53
    point size of 47
  downloadable 179
    "Unlimited Downloadable Fonts" 179
  formatting
    through the Ribbon 47
  installing
    importance of when printing from another Mac ! 181
  proportionally spaced 178
  screen 54
  using keyboard to select 54
Footer
  window for 79
Footers 78–79
  creating multiple 79
  current data icon for 78
  on first pages 79
  positioning 79
  setting
    in Print Preview 32
  style sheet for 79
Footnotes 131–137
  "Auto-numbered Reference" 132
  Continuation Notice 137
    dialog box 137
  Continuation Separator
    customizing 136
  determining where they should appear 134–135
  dialog box 132
  formatting 132, 133–134
  making an entry 132, 132–133
  numbering options 135
  removing 133
  Separators for 136
    customizing 136
  separators for 135–137
  split panes when working with 133
  window pane 133
Form letters. *See* Print merge
Format window
  Frame command in
    positioning text through 149
  positioning text through
    positioning text through 150
  selecting frames under 148
Formats
  file
    opening and saving other 200
    opening and saving *Word* 5.0 files in other 202
    unrecognized 202

Formats (continued)
  text
    opening and saving in various 201
Formatting
  data
    into tables 66
  footnotes 132, 133–134
  Index 128
    through Sections 131
    through Style Sheets 130–131
  Outlines 142–144
    through Style Sheets 142–144
  Sections 73
  Table of Contents 123–124
    as Section 124
  text 24, 46–55
    how to 53
    using the Character Command 53–55
"Fractional Widths" 178
Frames, 57
  anchoring them to reference points 150–153
  creating 104
  cropping and scaling 111
  dialog box for 151
  dragging 149
  fundamentals of 102–104
  inserting via the Ribbon 48
  "New Picture" button for creating 104
  positioning items using 148–153
  resizing without changing inner image 29
  selecting under Insert window vs. Format window 148
  white space around
    reducing or enlarging 149
  widths of
    resetting 150
"From Text" 58, 113
Front/Back tool 107
Functions
  customizing
    by adding to menus 210–211
    removing from menus 211

G

"General" (Preferences) 206–207
Glossaries 96–98
  built-in entries to 98
  creating entries for 96
  dialog box 97, 98
  editing ! 98
  inserting entries into 97
    keyboard shortcuts for 97
  merging files in 99
  multiple files 98–99

Glossaries (continued)
   opening a new file for 99
   saving
      a new file in 99
      changes to ! 97
   "Standard Entries" 98
   "Standard Glossary" file 98
Grade Level statistics 88
Grammar checker 85–87
   "Catch" 87
   customizing 86–87
      rule groups for 86–87
   dialog box 85
   Document statistics in 87–88
   Explain button 86
   Explanation dialog box 86
   finding and fixing bad grammar with 85–86
   ignoring advice in 86
   keyboard commands with ! 86
   manual changes in 86
   Preferences
      "Rule Groups" 87
   Readability statistics in 88
   turning off ! 87
"Graphic Files" 35
Graphics. *See also* Borders; Frames
   accessing frequently used
      through glossaries 96–98
   applying simple 111–113
   applying to tables 69
   borders
      dialog box for 112
   changing 105–107
   cropping 111
   deleting 108
   distorted imported
      preventing ! 111
   framing 102
      horizontal alignment for 151
   from other software programs
      cutting, copying, and pasting 189–191
      importing 109–110
   fundamentals of 102–103
   inline 102–103
   lines (rules)
      dialog box for 112
   manipulating 105, 111–113
      sizing handles for 111
   moving 105
   positioning 148–153
      on an anchored reference point 150–153
   PostScript
      "Print PostScript Over Text" 179

Graphics (continued)
   repeatedly used
      making easily accessible 50
      storing in Glossary ! 106
   resizing 105, 111
   resizing frames of 29
   scaling 111
   shading
      dialog box for 112
   smoothing
      when printing from LaserWriter 178
   tools 105–107
   un-positioning ! 149
   using Clipboard to import 109–110
   using Scrapbook to import 109–110
   using "Select All" with 108
   versatile placement of through tables 103
"Graphics Files" 109
Gray
   shading with 115
Grayscale
   printing from a LaserWriter 175
Gunning Fog Index 88
Gutters
   how to allow for 75

H

Handles
   for controlling graphics 111
Hanging indent 51
Header
   window for 79
Headers 78–79
   creating multiple 79
   current data icon for 78
   field
      adding to data documents 162–163
   on first pages 79
   positioning 79, 148
   setting
      in Print Preview 32
   style sheet for 79
Heading styles
   using to format Table of Contents ! 122
Headings
   aligning items to 152
   demoting
      icons for 140
   families in Outlines
      cross as symbol of 141
      promoting and demoting 141
   in Outlines 138
      adding numbers to 143–144
      box character as symbol for 139
      collapsing and expanding 141, 141–142

Headings (continued)
    entering 139
    promoting and demoting 139
    rearranging 140–142
    symbols for families in 139, 141
  levels of
    assigning them in Outline 138–139
  promoting and demoting
    icons for 139
Helmut's Dictionary 83
Help
  dialog box 42
  Online 42–43
    Balloon Help icon 43
    cancelling the question mark 43
    getting specific 43
Hidden style
  in Character Command 55
Horizontally
  aligning frames 151–152
  flipping pages
    in LaserWriter Options 179
"Hyphenate All" 90
  problems with 91
"Hyphenate Selection" 90
Hyphenation 90
  automatic 90
  buttons
    differences between 91
  dialog box 91
  "Hyphenate All" 90
    problems with 91
  preferences 209
  semi-automatic 91

I
.i. 126, 127
I-beam 23
Icons
  Balloon Help 43
  column sizing 76
  columns 47
  current data for header or footer 78
  double-arrow
    as heading demoter in Outline 140
  for promoting and demoting headings 139
  in Print Preview 32
  page numbering 77
  picture frame for graphics 47
  printer driver files 172
  text formatting character display 47
  Word 5.0 files 21
Identification screen
  for *Word* 5.0 22

IF... statements 166
"Ignore All"
  in Spelling checker 83
"Ignore Words in UPPERCASE" 84
"Ignore Words with Numbers" 84
ImageWriters
  documents prepared on
    when printing to a LaserWriter ! 181
  feeding
    envelopes into 183
  Options specific to 180
  options specific to 175–176
  Page Setup dialog box for 180
  paper options for 176
Importing
  data from other programs 161–163
  graphics from other programs 109–110
  with Publish and Subscribe 110
"Include Formatted Text in Clipboard"
  (Preferences) 207
Indent markers
  in the Ruler 50
Indents
  first line 51
  hanging 51
  left 51
  margin 49
    in Paragraph Command 57
  setting 50–51
Index 125–130
  choosing alphabetical headings for 128–129
  codes 126, 127
    for arguments 129
  codes for 125
  compiling 128–129
    the best time to do it ! 128
  cross-references 130
  entries
    combining with Table of Contents 127–128
    creating 126–127
    not directly in your text 126–127
  example of 125
  formatting
    nested and run-in 128
    through Sections 131
    using a Style Sheet 130–131
    using arguments for 129
  page numbers
    formatting 129
  page ranges
    indicating 129
  subentries 127

Information
  sharing with other software. *See also* Embedding; Linking; Publish and Subscribe
    the easy way   188–190
Inline graphics   102–103
Insert menu
  selecting frames under   148
Insert Table
  dialog box   65
Installing *Word* **5.0**   21
Interchange Format (RTF)
  opening and saving in   201
Italic type style
  choosing through the Ribbon   47

J

Jams, paper
  when merging documents   165
Joining
  text and graphics
    to an anchored reference point   150–153

K

"Keep Lines Together"   57
"Keep With Next"   57
Keyboard
  commands
    finding which ones are in use !   212
    in the Grammar checker !   86
    in the Thesaurus !   90
    making your own   42
    using with Spelling checker !   84
  shortcuts   41–42
    adding   212
    for inserting entries into glossaries   97
    removing   213
  using to move text cursor   27
  using to select text   26
keyboard
  shortcuts
    customizing   212–213

L

Labels, mailing. *See also* Print merge
  merging   166–167
Landscape mode   177
  for printing envelopes   183
"Larger Print Area"   179
LaserWriters   176
  cutting off text and graphics
    how to solve problem of !   178
  Options
    dialog box   179

LaserWriters (continued)
  Page Setup
    dialog box   177
    Options in   177–179, 179
  paper options for   176
  Print dialog box for   174
  printer driver
    for printing to disk   184–185
  printing documents on
    when prepared on ImageWriter !   181
  printing options specific to   175
Leaders (tab)
  setting
    through Paragraph Command   57
Letter spacing
  in Character Command   54
"Level" (Table of Contents)   122
Line and Fill tools   108
Line endings
  on screen
    not coinciding with what you see   178
Line Numbers   58
  determining position of   58
  dialog box   58
  viewing   59
Line spacing
  custom   56
  in Paragraph Command   56
Line styles   112
Line tool   106
Line width tool   107
Lines. *See also* Borders; Rules
  as rules
    dialog box for   112
  Continuation Separator (footnotes)   136
  numbering   58
  spacing of
    from the Ruler   49
Link Options dialog box   196
Linking   144–145
  dialog box for   144
  documents   195–196
    numbering items across a series of   145
    printing   145, 185–186
  drawbacks to   195
  Options for
    dialog box   196
  outlines to main document   137
  text
    editing   200
  with *Excel* 3.0   195
  with *QuickSwitch*
    updating and canceling   199–200
  with System 6   199

Links
  creating 195
  editing 196–197
  updating and canceling 195–196
  with *QuickSwitch*
    creating 199
"List Files of Type" 35
"List Recently Opened Documents" 35
Logical progression. *See* Outlines

M

***MacPaint* files**
  importing 109
  preventing distortions of ! 111
MacRecorder
  using in *Word* 5.0 153
MacWrite
  opening and saving in 200
***MacWrite* II**
  opening and saving in 200
Magnifying glass
  in Print Preview 31
Mailing labels. *See also* Print merge
  merging 166–167
  merging and printing 167
  preformatted label files
    adjustments to make on 166–167
    for printing 166
"Mailing Labels ReadMe" 166
Main documents
  creating
    with data document 163
  creating from Data document 163
  creating from existing data document 164
  in Print Merge 159
  merging
    with data 164–165
"Make Backup" 34
Manual changes
  in Grammar checker 86
Margin indents 49
  in Paragraph command 57
Margins
  as gutters 75
  changing in select paragraphs ! 75
  controlling for printing 176
  for printing envelopes 183
  markers for
    in the Ruler 50
  printing text and graphics in ! 74
  setting 74, 74–75
    for printing 177
    in Print Preview 32
    visually 75
"Match Case" 94

"Match Whole Word" 93
Math functions 156
"Meanings For" (Thesaurus) 89
Meanings of words
  using Thesaurus to get 89
Memory
  needed for running *Word* 5.0 20
Menu commands
  keyboard shortcuts for 41
Menus
  creating new 212
  customizing 210–212
    by adding functions 210–211
    example of 210
    removing functions 211
  items in
    quickly adding or removing 211–212
"Menus" (View Preferences) 208
"Merge and Print Results" 165
"Merge and Save Results in New File" 165
Merging
  cells
    in tables 68
  documents 164–165. *See also* Print Merge
    problems with 165
  glossary files 99
  mailing labels 166–167, 167
  file to read before 166
Microphone
  using in *Word* 5.0 153–155
"Mirror Even/Odd" 75
Misspellings
  finding and correcting 82
Mistakes
  undoing 25–26
Modifying styles (in Style Sheets) 62–63
Moving. *See also* Dragging
  around a document 26–27
  by keyboard 27
  text 25
    "drag and drop" method 25
  voice annotations ! 154
MultiFinder
  the Clipboard with 189
Multiple documents
  printing 174
Multiple windows 40
Multiplying 156
Music
  making customized in *Word* 5.0 153–155

N

Nested Index formatting 128
"New Picture" 104

"Next Style" 62
"No Gaps Between Pages" (Printing) 180
Normal view
    headers and footers in 79
    inability to see positioning in ! 148
    limitations of 30
"Not in Dictionary" 82
Numbering
    footnotes
        options for 135
    items across a series of linked documents 145
    lines 58
    pages 77–78
        formatting 77–78
    paragraphs 59–60
        by example 60
        formatting for 59
        multilevel 59–60
        updating 60
    Sections 73, 78
Numbers
    calculating 156–157
    heading in Outlines
        adding 143–144
Numerically arranging information 157–158

O

Objects
    embedding 197–198
        creating new from empty 198
        editing 199
Online Help 42–43
    cancelling the question mark 43
    getting specific 43
"Only Check for Errors" 165
"Open and Save" (Preferences) 208–209
"Open Documents" (View Preferences) 208
Opening
    dictionaries 83
    existing documents 34–35
    glossary files 99
    in other file formats 200–202
    new documents 22
    Word 5.0 files
        in other file formats 202
Options
    dialog box
        example of LaserWriter's 179
    for printing
        in Page Setup 176–177

Options (continued)
    ImageWriter 180
    in Spelling checker 84
    LaserWriter 179
    printing 174–176
Organizing your ideas. *See* Outlines
Orientation
    page
        controlling for printing 176
        how to set a new default for 74
        setting 74
Outline view 32
Outlines 137–143
    accessing 137
    adding body text to
        from another view 140
    adding text to 139–140
    as related to documents 138
    command bar in 142
    formatting 142–144
        using Style Sheets for 142–144
    heading families in
        promoting and demoting 141
        symbols for 139
    headings in 138
        adding numbers to 143–144
        assigning levels 138–139
        box character as symbol for 139
        collapsing and expanding 141–142
        entering 139
        promoting and demoting 139, 140
    making a Table of Contents from 122–123
    rearranging 140–142
    starting 138–139
    using Style Sheets to format 142–144
    using to create multiple reference tables 124
    view 138
        example of 138

P

"Page Break Before" 57
Page breaks 27–28
    automatic 27
    "Background Repagination" 28
    controlling 28
    controlling through Paragraph command 57
    examples of 28
    manual (hard) 28
        deleting 28
    "Repaginate Now" 28
    repagination 28
Page design. *See* Positioning

Page Layout view 30–31
   checking document in before printing
     reasons for ! 175
   disadvantages of 31
   headers and footers in 79
   positioning items in ! 148
   resizing columns in 76
   selecting 30
   setting as default 31
   text formatting characters in
     as seen in Section feature 73

Page numbering
   icon for 77

Page numbers 77–78
   formatting 77
   in Sections 78
   Index
     formatting 129
   placing in Print Preview 31
   starting in File Series dialog box 186

Page ranges
   in Index
     indicating 129
   printing in linked documents 185–186

Page Setup
   controlling printing from 176–180
   dialog box
     for the ImageWriter 180
     for the LaserWriter 177
   options
     general 176–177
     specific to the LaserWriter 177–179

Pages
   choosing specific to print 173
   current
     how to find the number of 28
   edge
     printing as close to as possible 179
   facing
     how to set 75
   first
     determining different headers and
     footers for 79
   flipping horizontally
     in LaserWriter Options 179
   flipping vertically
     in LaserWriter Options 179
   margins for 74–75
   margins of
     setting for printing 177
   orientation of 74
     controlling for printing 176
     setting for printing 177
   printing
     options for 175
     setting up 176–180

Pages (continued)
   printing backwards
     fixing the problem of ! 175
   single or facing
     viewing in Print Preview 32
   size of
     setting 74
     setting custom when printing 177

Pagination 27–28. *See also* Page breaks
   in Paragraph Command 57
   repagination 28

Panes
   splitting document windows into 39–40
   working in different modes 40

Paper
   controlling printing size of 176
   types of
     choosing for printing 176

Paper jams
   when merging documents
     what to do 165

"Paper Source" (Printing) 175

Paragraph
   attributes
     finding and replacing 95
   numbering
     updating 60
   spacing of
     from the Ruler 49
   specific formatting
     from the Ruler ! 49

Paragraph button (in the Ribbon) 48

Paragraph Command 55–57
   apply button in 57
   dialog box 56
   leaders (tab) in 57
   line spacing in 56
   margin indents in 57
   pagination in 57
   paragraph spacing in 56
   tabs in 57

Paragraph marks 23
   turning on and off 23

Paragraphs
   numbering 59–60
     by example 60
     dialog box 60
     multilevel 59–60
   setting tabs in 52
   sorting 158

Parenthesis
   numbers in
     Word 5.0's special treatment of 156–157

Paste up
   mechanical. *See* Positioning

Pasting
    information from other software programs 188–191
    text 25
    with graphics 108
Patterns (drawing)
    examples of 108
Percentages
    computing 156
PICT files
    importing 109
PICT2 files
    importing 109
"Picture" (Insert) 109
Picture button 48
"Picture Placeholders" (View Preferences) 207–208
Playing
    sound annotations 155
Plug-in modules 21
Point size of type
    choosing in the Ribbon 47
Polygon tool 106
Portrait mode (Printing) 177
Position box
    in Character Command 54
Positioning
    alignments for 151–153
    graphics
        horizontally 151–152
        vertically 152
    items
        aligning them to text 152–153
    page view for ! 148
    text
        horizontally 151–152
        through Format window 149, 150
        vertically 152
    text and graphics 148–153
        to an anchored reference point 150–153
        un-positioning ! 149
PostScript files
    as printer's destination 175
    importing 109
    "Print PostScript Over Text" 179
    printing to disk 184–185
Power sharing
    a quick overview 188
Practice documents 21
"Precision Bitmap Alignment" 179
Preferences 206–209
    changing measurement in the ruler 49
    custom page sizes 74
    customizing page sizes from 177

Preferences (continued)
    dialog box 87, 207
    hyphenation 209
    in Spelling checker 84
    restoring *Word* 5.0's original 214
    "Rule Groups" 87
    saving multiple files of ! 206
    saving your customized 213–214
    setting 206
    Thesaurus 209
    those available 206–209
"Print Back to Front" 175
"Print Hidden Text" 175
Print Merge 158–165
    command 164
    "Data Document Builder" dialog box 160
    data documents in 159
        creating 160
    dialog box 165
    Helper bar 164
    Helper feature 158
    main documents in 159
    problems with 165
"Print Next File" 175
"Print PostScript Over Text" 179
Print Preview view 31–32
    adjusting pages within 31
    choosing 31
    example of 31
    icons in 32
    magnifying glass in 31
    making corrections in 31
    numbering pages through 77
    placing page numbers in 31, 31–32
    setting headers or footers in 32
    setting margins in 32
        visually 75
    sudden screen shifts to 150
    using before printing 38
    viewing
        line numbers in 59
        single or facing pages in 32
"Print:" (on LaserWriter) 175
Printer drivers
    LaserWriter
        for printing to disk 184–185
Printers. *See also* ImageWriters; LaserWriters
    avoiding confusion among 181
    distinctions among when printing mailing labels 166
    drivers for 172
    icons of 172
    memory
        downloaded fonts and 179
    setting up 172

Printers (continued)
    switching   181
Printing   172–183
    a list of *Word* 5.0's commands !   213
    a quick overview   38
    a selection of text   174
    as close to the edge as possible   179
    backwards
        fixing !   175
    basics   173–175
    checking document before !   175
    choosing types of paper for   176
    envelopes   182–183
        addressing   182–183
        how to feed into a LaserWriter   183
        margins for   183
        templates for !   183
        using Landscape mode for   183
    example of dialog box for   174
    from Print Preview   32
    in the margins !   74
    line endings
        not coinciding with what's on the screen   178
    linked documents   145, 185–186
    mailing labels   166, 166–167, 167
    making default settings for   177
    multiple documents   174
    on a different Mac than you created on
        installing fonts when !   181
    options   174–176
        specific to the ImageWriter   175–176
        specific to the LaserWriter   175
    Page Setup
        dialog box for the LaserWriter   177
    pages
        a range of in linked documents   185–186
        choosing specific   173
        customizing sizes for   177
        options for   175
        setting orientation for   177
    "Paper Source"   175
    Postscript files to disk   184–185
    "Print Hidden Text"   175
    "Print Next File"   175
    role of Chooser in   172–173
    sections
        a range of !   73
    setting up pages for   176–180
    with different printers   180–181
Program file
    Word 5.0's   21
Programs
    other software
        placing *Word* 5.0 files into   203

"Prompt for Summary Info"   36, 208–209
Proportionally spaced fonts   178
Publish and Subscribe   191–194
    a brief overview   191
    "Editions"   191
        subscribing to   193
    importing with   110
    "Publisher"
        creating   191–192
        updating and canceling   192–193
    Subscriber Options dialog box   194
    "Subscribers"
        editing   194
        updating and canceling   193–194
"Publisher"   191
    creating   191–192
    updating and canceling   192–193

Q

"Quality" (Printing)   175
QuickSwitch
    creating links with   199
    editing text in   200
    linking data with   199
    updating and canceling links with   199–200
    using to share information !   191
    why to graduate from !   199

R

Ranges, page
    Index
        indicating   129
Ranges, pages
    printing in linked documents   185–186
Readability statistics   88
    skipping   88
"Readable Files"   35
Rearranging
    outlines   140, 140–142
Recording
    voice annotations   153–155
        quickly   154
Rectangle tool   106
Redoing   26
"Reduce or Enlarge" (Printing)   177
Reference tables
    creating multiple   124–125
Removing
    items in a menu
        quickly   211–212
"Renumber"   59
"Repaginate Now"   28
Replace. *See* Find and Replace
Requirements
    for using *Word* 5.0   20

Resetting
   text frame widths   150
Return key   22
   when not to use   22
   when to use   22
Ribbon   46, 47–48
   command bar for   24
   creating graphic frames from   104
   example of   47
   Picture button in   48, 104
   setting columns from   76
   setting varied columns in   77
   when making tables !   65
Rich Text Format   208
   opening and saving in   201
Rotate tool   106
Rounded rectangle tool   106
Rows
   adding   156
   applying borders and lines to   113
   in Tables
      adding and deleting   67
      sorting   157–158
RTF   208
   opening and saving in   201
"Rule Groups"   87
Ruler   46, 48–50
   changing measurement preferences of   49
   command bar for   24
   example of   48
   extensive formatting effects of !   49
   indents in
      setting   50–52
   line and paragraph spacing in   49
   margin indents in   49
      setting   50–51
   margins indents in
      changing for select paragraphs !   75
   paragraph-specific formatting in !   49
   table markers in   50
   tabs markers in   49–50
      setting   52–53
   text alignment in   49
   when making Tables !   65
Rules (lines)
   applying   111–112
Run-in Index formatting   128

S

Sample Documents   21
   folder
      preformatted label files in   166
"Save As"
   using to avoid massive files   34
   initially   33

"Save File as Type"   202, 33
Saving
   any customizations you've made   213–214
   documents   33–34
      "Fast Save"   34
      for the first time   33
      for use in other word processing
        programs   33–34
      "Make Backup"   34
      "Save File as Type"   33
      subsequent times   34
   documents before sorting
      importance of !   157
   glossary files   99
   in other file formats   200–202
   Word 5.0 files
      in other file formats   202
Scaling graphics   111
Scrapbook
   permanent storage of information in   190
   using to import graphics   109–110
   using to share information with other
      programs   189–191
Screen
   suddenly shifting to different view   150
Screen fonts   54
Search and Replace *See also* Find and
     Replace
   special characters in
      formatting codes for   95
Searching for files. *See* Find File
Secondary entries
   Index   127
"Section Break"   72
Sections   72–73
   applying formats to   73
   creating   72
   deleting   73
   dialog box   73
   first pages in
      determining different headers and
        footers for   79
   Format menu in
      setting columns from   76
   formatting Index in   131
   how to tell which one you're in   73
   numbering   73
   page numbers in   78
   "Section Break"   72
   Table of Contents as
      formatting   124
   using to vary columns   77
"See" (in Index)   130
"Select All"   26
   with graphics   108

Selecting
   dictionaries   83
   text
      a large range of   26
      on a limited basis   26
      tips for   26
      using the keyboard for   26
Selection tool   105
Semi-automatic hyphenation   91
Separators
   for footnotes   135–137
Series
   of documents
      linking   144–145
Settings
   restoring *Word* 5.0's original   214
Settings file   214
   box   214
   creating   214
   opening   214
Shading   115
   applying   111
   dialog box for accessing   112
   in Tables   69
Shapes. *See* Graphics
Sharing *See also* Embedding; Publish and Subscribe; Linking
   information
      with System 7 !   191
   power
      a quick overview   188
Shortcuts
   keyboard   41–42
      adding   212
      customizing   212–213
      removing   213
"Show" (View Preferences)   207–208
"Show Clipboard"   110
"Show Document Statistics"   87
"Show Page Numbers" (Table of Contents)   122
Size of type
   choosing   53
Sizing handles
   for manipulating graphics   111
"'Smart' Quotes" (Preferences)   207
Smoothing
   text and graphics
      when printing from LaserWriter   178
Software.
   sharing information with other   188–203
Sorting   157–158
   example of   158
   paragraphs   158
   saving documents before
      importance of !   157

Sorting (continued)
   tabbed data   158
Sound
   making through voice annotations   153–155
   playing   155
   quality of
      regulating in voice annotations   154–155
Space bar
   when not to use for alignment   22
Space, hhite
   around frames
      reducing or enlarging   149
Spacing
   letter
      in Character Command   54
   line and paragraph
      from the Ruler   49
   paragraph
      in Paragraph Command   56
Speaker symbol
   showing and hiding !   155
Speaking
   into your Mac through *Word* 5.0   153–155
Special characters
   formatting code for   95
   in Find and Replace   94–95
Spelling. *See* Spelling checker
"Spelling" (Preferences)   209
Spelling checker   82–84
   correcting mistakes made in !   83
   dialog box   82
   finding and correcting misspellings in   82
   "Ignore All"   83
   "Ignore Words in UPPERCASE"   84
   "Ignore Words with Numbers"   84
   "Not in Dictionary"   82
   options in   84
   unrecognized spellings in   83
   using keyboard commands with !   84
Split bar   39–40
Split panes
   with footnotes   133
Splitting
   document windows   39–40
   undoing   40
Spreadsheet
   how *Word* 5.0 is not a !   156
"Standard Entries" (Glossary)   98
"Standard Glossary" file   98
"Start At"   59
Start button (Section dialog box)   73
Starting *Word* 5.0   21
Stationery
   saving documents as forms for   201

Statistics
    readability   88
    skipping   88
Style of type
    choosing
        through the Ribbon   47–48
    in Character Command   54, 55
Style Sheets   61–62
    applying   62
        using keyboard commands !   62
    "Based On"   62
    basing one style on another   61–62
    building borders and lines into !   113
    button in the Ruler for selecting styles
        from   49
    copying from other documents   63
    creating   61–62
    creating your own default from !   63
    "Define" button in creating   61
    dialog box   62
    finding and replacing styles from   96
    footer   79
    formatting footnotes with   133–134
    formatting Index through   130–131
    formatting Table of Contents
        through   123–124
    header   79
    heading styles in
        using to format Table of Contents !   122
    in tables !   66
    modifying
        based on a text selection   63
    modifying styles in   62–63
    "Next Style"   62
    on-screen display for current paragraph   63
    prebuilt styles in *Word* 5.0   63
    redefining. *See* Styles, modifying
    using to format Outlines   142–144
Styles (text formatting). *See* Style Sheet
Subentries
    Index   127
"Subscribe To"   193
Subscriber Options dialog box   194
"Subscribers"   191. *See also* Publish and
    Subscribe
    editing   194
    updating and canceling   193–194
Subscribing. *See* Publish and Subscribe
Subscript
    formatting through the Ribbon   48
    in Character Command   54
Subtracting   156
    figures in parenthesis   156
"Summary Info"
    dialog box   36
    turning on and off   36

Summary Information
    prompting for   208–209
Superscript
    formatting through the Ribbon   48
    in Character Command   54
Symbols. *See also* Icons
    for heading families in Outlines   139
    speaker
        showing and hiding !   155
Synonyms   89
System 7
    a pitch for !   199
    and sharing information !   191
    balloon help   43
    embedding with   197
    linking capabilities of   195
    "Publish and Subscribe" in   110
    the Clipboard with   189
    using *Word* 5.0 with   20–21
System requirements for *Word* 5.0   20–21
Linking
    QuickSwitch for   199
System 6
    linking with   199
    QuickSwitch with
        for linking data   199
    the Clipboard with   189
    why to upgrade from !   199

T

Tab
    "delimited" text   65
Tabbed data
    sorting   158
Table
    shading   115
"Table gridlines" (View Preferences)   207–208
"Table Layout" dialog box   68
Table markers
    in the Ruler   50
Table of Contents   118–124
    codes   127
        in creating multiple tables   124–125
        inserting   119–120
        viewing through Preferences !   120
    "Collect"   121
    compiling   121–122
    creating entries for   119–121
    creating multiple   124–125
    dialog box   121
    entries
        combining with Index   127–128
        multilevel   120–121

Table of Contents (continued)
   example of   118
   formatting   123–124
      as Sections   124
      through Style Sheets   123–124
   importance of recompiling !   122
   "Level"   122
   making entries not in the text   120
   making from an outline   122–123
   multilevel entries
      codes   121
   multiple
      choosing "No" when creating   125
   removing entries !   120
   "Show Page Numbers"   122
   using heading styles to format !   122

Tables   64–68
   aligning   68
   applying borders and lines to   113
   applying borders to
      what to do when complicated   113–115
   Border command   69
   cells
      dialog box   67, 69
   columns in
      adding and deleting   67
      resizing   67
   converting existing text into   65
   creating   65–66
   dialog box   65
   entering and formatting data into   66
   examples of   64
   framing   69
   graphics in   69
   Insert Table
      dialog box   65
   merging cells in   68
   modifying   67–68
   polishing   69
   positioning   148–153
   rows in
      adding and deleting   67
      sorting   157–158
   shading in   69
   "Table Layout" dialog box   68
   "Text to Table"   65
   using style sheets with   66
   using to place graphics   103
   why not to use tabs when making   64

Tables, reference
   creating multiple   124–125

Tabs
   changing kinds of !   53
   deleting   53
   in data documents
      using to move from cell to cell   161

Tabs (continued)
   leaders with
      setting in Paragraph Command   57
   markers for
      in the Ruler   49–50
   moving   53
   moving among   52
   removing   53
      through Paragraph Command   57
   setting   52–53
      through Paragraph Command   57
   when to use and when not to use   53
   why not to use hhen making tables   64

"Tall Adjusted"   180

Templates
   creating   201
   for envelopes !   183

Text
   accessing frequently used
      through glossaries   96–98
   adding to Outlines   139–140
   aligning items to   152
   alignment
      from the Ruler   49
   attributes of
      finding and replacing   95–96
   converting
      existing text into tables   65
      into graphics !   107
   deselecting !   26
   editing   25–26
   Find and Replace   93
   formats
      opening and saving in various   201
   formatting   24, 46–55
      how to   53
      using the Character Command   53–55
   frames
      resetting widths of   150
   framing
      horizontal alignment for   151
   from other software programs
      cutting, copying, and pasting   189–191
   moving in a document   25
   positioning   148–153
      on an anchored reference point   150–153
      through Format menu   149, 150
   printing a selection of   174
   selecting
      a large range of   26
      tips for   26
      using the keyboard   26
   selecting limited   26
   shading   115

Text (continued)
   smoothing
      when printing from LaserWriter 178
   un-positioning ! 149
Text Alignment tool 107
"Text and Graphics Smoothing" 178
"Text Boundaries..." (View Preferences) 207–208
Text cursor
   positioning 23
Text files (ASCII) 162
Text formatting characters 23
   showing from the Ribbon 48
   turning on and off 23
"Text Only" format
   opening and saving in 201
"Text Only With Line Breaks" format
   opening and saving in 201
"Text to Table" 65
Text tool 106
"Text With Layout" format
   opening and saving in 201
Text wrap 22, 148, 149
Thesaurus 89
   coaxing suggestions from ! 89
   dialog box 89
   keyboard commands with ! 90
   "Meanings For" 89
   preferences 209
   replacing words using 89
TIFF files
   importing 109
   preventing distortions of ! 111
Title bar
   in document windows 39
   using to move a window on screen 39
Title screen
   for *Word* 5.0 22
TOC. *See* Table of Contents
Tools
   drawing palette 105–107
Trimming graphics. *See* Cropping graphics
TrueType 54
Type. *See* Character Command; Style of type
Typing
   how to in *Word* 5.0 22
   keyboard shortcuts 41–42. *See also* Keyboard

U

Underline
   choosing through the Ribbon 47
   in Character Command 54
Undoing 25–26
   redoing 26

Ungrammatical phrasings. *See* Grammar checker
"Unlimited Downloadable Fonts" 179
Updating
   links 195–196
   "Publisher" 192–193
"Use As Default"
   ! 63
   for setting new page default size and orientation 74

V

Versions
   of software
      opening and saving in 200–202
Vertically
   aligning
      text and graphics 152
   flipping pages
      in LaserWriter Options 179
"View" (Preferences) 207
Viewing documents 29–31
   default view 29
   in multiple windows 40
   Normal view 29–30
      example of 29
   Outline view 32
   Page Layout view 30–31
      selecting 30–31
   Print Preview view 31–32
   sudden screen shifts while 150
Views
   outline 138
Voice annotations 153–155
   moving them around a document ! 154
   recording 153–155
      quickly 154
   regulating sound quality of 154–155
   speaker symbol in
      showing and hiding ! 155

W

Width of line
   tool for setting 107
Window pane
   footnote 133
Windows. *See also* Dialog boxes
   header and footer 79
Windows, document. *See* Document windows
Windows, multiple. *See* Multiple windows
***Word* (*Microsoft*)**
   opening and saving versions other than *Word* 5.0 200

Word count 91–92
    dialog box 92
Word folder
    what's in it 21
Word processing programs
    saving documents for use in other 33–34
WordPerfect
    opening and saving in 201
Words
    meanings of 89
Works (Microsoft)
    adding data from 161–162
    opening and saving in 200
Wrapping text 148, 149

(that's all, folks!)

Colophon

The Little Mac Word Book is, as you might expect, a 100% Macintosh production. I drafted chapters with Microsoft Word 4.0, and later moved up to a beta version of Word 5.0 (when it seemed stable). Chapter layouts were produced with Aldus PageMaker 4.01, running on my System 7-equipped Macintosh IIcx, with 5 megabytes of RAM, and a 90 megabyte hard drive. (If you ever produce a book via Macintosh, I strongly recommend this type of configuration as a bare *minimum*.) Page proofs sputtered out of my ancient PS Jet PostScript laser printer, while final output was handled by a sleek Linotronic 300 imagesetter. The main fonts used are the ITC New Baskerville and Futura families, both from Adobe Systems, Inc.

Credit for this book's beautiful design goes to Robin Williams, author of the one-and-only *Little Mac Book* (also from Peachpit Press); copy editing by Kimn Neilson; index by Mary Grady; cover design by Studio Silicon; typesetting by Fifth Street Computer Services.